C000131994

'"There's no short-cut" they used to say, but Pippa has sneakily written one. Whether you're already performing and want a guide to get you out of your head, or if you secretly wish you could be more creative – this book is for you. Pippa knows what is holding you back and if you want to be more present, more reactive and have more fun – this book is for you!'

Sara Pascoe, author of *Animal* and *Sex, Power, Money*

'Pippa is one of the greatest improvisers I've ever seen on stage. To be in a show with her is a joy, to be taught by her is a privilege and now to have her thoughts all written down to digest, is a triumph. Essential reading for anyone wanting to do life, but better'

Cariad Lloyd, performer and presenter of *Griefcast*

'Funny, insightful and inspiring. This book will make you question yourself in the best possible way. Brings improv into your everyday life; this book really will change your life.'

Rachel Parris, writer and performer of BBC2's *The Mash Report*

IMPROV YOUR LIFE

PIPPA EVANS

HODDER*studio*

First published in Great Britain in 2021 by Hodder Studio
An Imprint of Hodder & Stoughton
An Hachette UK Company

1 3 5 7 9 10 8 6 4 2

Copyright © Pippa Evans, 2021

The right of Pippa Evans to be identified as the Author of the Work has been
asserted by them in accordance with the Copyright, Designs and Patents Act 1988.

All rights reserved. No part of this publication may be reproduced, stored
in a retrieval system, or transmitted, in any form or by any means without
the prior written permission of the publisher, nor be otherwise circulated
in any form of binding or cover other than that in which it is published and
without a similar condition being imposed on the subsequent purchaser.

A CIP catalogue record for this book is
available from the British Library.

ISBN (Trade Paperback) 978 1 5293 4485 1
ISBN (eBook) 978 1 5293 4486 8
ISBN (Audio) 9 781 5293 4487 5

Typeset in Caecilia by Hewer Text UK Ltd, Edinburgh
Printed and bound in Great Britain by Clays Ltd, Elcograf S.p.A.

Hodder & Stoughton policy is to use papers that are natural, renewable
and recyclable products and made from wood grown in sustainable
forests. The logging and manufacturing processes are expected to
conform to the environmental regulations of the country of origin.

Hodder & Stoughton Ltd
Carmelite House
50 Victoria Embankment
London EC4Y 0DZ

www.hodder-studio.com

For Mum and Dad
who lay the platform.

My brothers, Charlie, Sam and Benjy
who have been my sidekicks (and antagonists)
along the way.

And my permanent YES AND – Mr Bunce.

CONTENTS

WELCOME

Hello. I am Pippa Evans and I am an improviser. I teach it, I perform it and I LOVE IT. I do it on stage in the West End with *Showstopper! The Improvised Musical*, in tiny rooms above pubs with friends and over Zoom with my friends' kids. I teach it to excited students, ready to play and explore, and in corporate boardrooms with less-enthusiastic-to-begin-with lawyers and marketing executives. I teach it at festivals all around the world, and I am fascinated by the ways in which improvisation can elicit the most extraordinary joy from a few people standing on a stage just listening and responding to each other.

You've probably heard of improvisation, or watched a clip of *Whose Line Is It Anyway* on YouTube, or had an awkward 30-minute drama lesson at school – where Mr Hargreaves tried to make you stand in front of the whole class and pretend to be a talking potato and you wanted to curl up and die. Or maybe your company forced you onto an away day which you thought was going to be all beer and raft-building but instead there were five actors wearing matching t-shirts and your ass clamped up. Sorry about that – I was probably one of those actors. If you've had a not-so-shiny experience with improv*, I would like to assure you that it was simply a blip in the improv universe. Improv is the best, especially when you are doing it.

Why? Because the best improv experience is not had watching it (that is a different kind of magic). It is in the workshop space, where you are a part of the improvisation, rather than the audience enjoying the process. Great improvisation on stage is done by brilliant performers who also work as actors/writers/comedians/singers. What you are watching is a group of people who already have skills using the conduit of improvisation to create brilliant theatrical experiences. Which is why I believe improvisation should be studied by everyone – because it brings out the best in us all, no matter our profession, our status or our experience of the world. Those who engage with improvisation will get more out of life.

There.

I said it.

Are you still here?

Good.

If I had to release a manifesto, it would be that every child should have the opportunity to study improvisation from the age of ten until they leave school. Why ten? Because ten is when self-doubt and the outside world really start to creep into children's brains. I was once teaching in a primary school where I did a workshop with every single year group from four years old to eleven years old and I loved it. I pretended to be

---

* We can get into whether you say 'improv' or 'impro' but really, it's whichever falls off your tongue better.

butterflies with the littlest ones and played 'Creating New Insults' in the style of *The Twits* with the bigger ones (the best new insult was, 'You look like a spaghetti face'). But what made me sad was seeing the cynicism starting to appear. 'This is stupid,' said one girl (if this had been an improv scene, she would have been smoking a cigarette and tapping ash onto another kid's head), and her cynicism spread to half the class, who were then ashamed that they were actually quite liking it. And that cynicism is hard to shake, because we have been fed the lie that rejecting people's offers and not joining in is the cool choice. You get more respect if you belittle others; if you stay in the safe zone and judge everyone else.

I know that feeling. I have to fight it every day. The wish to sneer so that you're not left behind. I remember the first time I ever experienced improvisation and let that feeling stop me joining in. I was maybe eight years old and we were told there was a surprise for us waiting in the school hall. We were so excited! We lined up and got ready to go down the stairs, and when we walked in, we found a Scottish man with a big ginger beard. I grew up in London, so anyone who didn't sound like they were selling apples or had plums in their mouth was mega exciting. He asked me, 'How did you get to school today?' and I said, 'My mum drove me.' And he said, 'OK – now imagine a whole different way of getting to school!' And I thought for a bit and I said, 'I walked,' and he said, with a slight wince, 'OK, but how else might you have come to school today? If you could come any way at all?' I rolled my eyes, like I was too good for this crazy cat and said, 'I don't know, an elephant?' and his eyes lit up and he said, 'That's right! An elephant! All the way from India!', and he started stomping around the room like he was on an elephant. And I LOVED IT. But I pretended not to so that my classmates wouldn't think I was lame. And really, which is more lame? Oh sweet, little Pippa. How I wish I could shake you and say, 'Ride the elephant!' But I can't, and to this day, I wish I could find that Scottish man, apologise profusely, and then ride off into the distance together on an imaginary elephant.

This here is something we have to turn our attention to. Not joining in, on the most basic level, because we are worried about what people might think. That is poison right there. Forget about sugar in fizzy drinks – worrying what people might think is what's really killing us. It stops us taking part in so many moments when we know, deep down, that we want to. We feel the fizz in our bellies that we want to say something funny back in the staffroom, but we don't because it might not be funny out loud. We don't dance at our friend's wedding because we are self-conscious about our bodies being seen.

We fear people witnessing us being vibrant and free, in case there is a comment or a look that might hit us like a bullet and bleed that last tiny bit of confidence we were saving onto the dance floor and out of our lives.

Improv and Me

My first professional experience with improvisation came when I was 23. I was in a new (written) musical at the

Edinburgh Fringe Festival. I was playing a 55-year-old house-wife called Anya who was married to the ringmaster of a fail-ing circus. My first line was, 'Only ten people in tonight,' which was funny, because we never had more than four in the audi-ence. There was a clown in this circus, but he was depressed. I had to sing a song about my daughter getting an abortion. You can see why it might not have been a hot ticket.

To cheer myself up, I would go and watch an improv group called Improvedy, and I thought they were hilarious. I went back night after night, marvelling at their magic. I got to know the group, and they suggested that when we got back to London, I try improv out. Luckily, one member of the team* decided to leave the group on return to London, and so a space appeared for 'a girl' – because in those days you could only have one woman in a group: because even improvisers can be caught up in the 'But-where-will-the-men-go-if-boobs-take-up-all-the-space' arguments.

Since then, I have been in many, many improv groups. It's addictive, improv, so do be careful, because once you get involved, you cannot stop. The adrenaline rush of not know-ing what you are about to do is bonkers. I would love to compare the blood pressure of a bungee jumper to that of an improviser. Once, Showstopper was about to do a corporate performance for the *Britain's Got Talent* production team (yes, the judges were all in the room) and we all happened to be

---

* This lady who left was none other than madam Ruth Bratt, who has since become a best pal and fellow member of not one, but THREE, improv groups: Showstopper!, Yes Queens and The Glenda J Collective.

wearing Fitbits. Just before we went on, our wrists started vibrating – our heart rates were so high that the Fitbits were concerned for our health. Nice that they care, isn't it? Don't worry, we smashed it.

Working intensely in these improv groups (often it is as intense as it is fun), improvisers experience most emotions: love for each other, jealousy over skills and projects, anger towards behaviour, amazement at the beauty of someone's work, confusion when people don't do what you expected, sexual tension because you're all growing up together and fights about silly things like who gets the double bed in a Travelodge family room. But what stands out the most is the profound sense of connection we experience as a group. When we stand on stage, not knowing what is going to happen but spontaneously singing from the same hymn sheet (in the case of *Showstopper! The Improvised Musical*, literally), it is magical. And in those moments, you realise that every day is a beautiful bonkers experiment and you are just a molecule in the test tube of life.

It is, however, hard to be grateful for the wonder that is life when you are late for the bus, or your kids are only eating fish fingers this week and you've just finished the last box in the freezer, or Omar is stressing you out in team meetings. But let me tell you, these are the places where improv techniques can be unseen gifts, mini heroes that lift you out of a slump, shift your perspective and help you connect to where you are right in that moment rather than wishing you were somewhere else. It can kick-start your creativity, taking your imagination places you didn't know it could go. It can make failing ten times less scary – showing you that you can put your hand up in a meeting and follow your thought rather than prepare every contribution. It will help you play with your kids, listen to your family and notice yourself.

Improv cannot save your life, but it can help you feel more in control of your life, ironically*, by helping you let go of control. Say what? Don't worry, that's how I used to feel, too.

Would it help if I told you that I am a bit of a control freak? That I worry about what people think of me sometimes, and that I have been known to construct whole arguments to make my point weeks after the point wasn't made? Because all that is true. I left school thinking life should be a nice straight path of success and bluebirds landing on my hand as I charm everyone I meet. But it wasn't and they didn't.

Nothing ever happens like you think it will, and my 20s were riddled with self-doubt and self-loathing, even when on paper I was doing a great job working as a comedian. My 'doing well' didn't seem to be making me well. I was making weird choices, saying 'yes' to too many things and had a sneaking suspicion that at any moment, someone might realise that I was a fraud. That I wasn't a great performer. That I should really be in a cave in the darkness somewhere (no offence if you actually live in a cave) and that everyone who ever said, 'I love your work,' was just waiting to call me up and yell down the line, 'Finally. I can tell you what I actually think of you.'

---

* Is this ironic? Alanis confused me so much with that song.

I first realised this was becoming a problem when I couldn't stop crying for a week. I wasn't quite sure what was going on. It was worrying for me and my husband, who has lived with me for twelve years and therefore notices when half a bucket of water is pouring out of my face.

On paper, I had all the qualifications – TV and radio credits, invitations to international festivals, Joe Pasquale's phone number. But I didn't feel confident. I didn't feel like an award winner. I felt like a fraud and that I was going to ruin everything if I opened my mouth. I started having dreams about jumping in front of a bus. I had chest pains. It was dark, but I had so much to be grateful for that I didn't say anything for fear of looking like an attention seeker, or that people might realise I wasn't a super-human success story. Imagine the headlines, 'WOMAN ISN'T COPING' – I'd be letting everyone down.

Later that week, I had to take a trip to Cornwall. As the train pulled out of Paddington, the sun was streaming in the window and I felt a huge release, a weight lifting from me. I leant back and thought: 'It's all going to be alright.'

Just then, my phone beeped. It was my agent reminding me of a gig I had the next night in some far corner of the UK. I had not put it in my diary. I immediately started to panic and started weeping uncontrollably. There was no way I could do this gig in the state I was in. Also, I was in Cornwall. I reached in my bag for a tissue, but I didn't have one, so I had to dry my tears and blow my nose with the only thing to hand – a Christmas sock. Poor Rudolf.

I started berating myself for being such an idiot. I worried that my agent would scream at me (they have never screamed at me), that the comedy industry would say I was a flake (you could never describe me as a flake), that I would never get booked again (extreme reaction for a small club who are always pleased to see you), and I had no idea what to do.

Well, I *did* have an idea of what to do, but I was too worried about doing it. There were two Pippas at work. Anxious Pippa and calm, logical Pippa. We'll call them P1 (anxious) and P2 (calm). P2 said I should just reply and tell my agent what was going on. But P1 was worried my agent would sack me on the spot. After an hour of debate in my head, P2 managed to convince P1 that the first option was the right choice. So I wrote an email that just said:

'I'm really sorry – I can't stop crying and I am worried that something is very wrong. I think it might be anxiety or something. I can't do the gig. Please forgive me.'

My agent replied immediately.

'Have cancelled the gig and can cancel all other gigs if you need me to.'

Within 10 minutes all her associates had messaged me to check I was OK, to say they were sorry I was having such a bad time and, if I felt able, that I should come into the office on Monday to talk about how to move forward. So, no screaming. I felt immediately better for having just said what was going on instead of what I thought they wanted to hear. Lucky me, having such a supportive gang.

The lady behind me on the train offered me a tissue. Kind, but surprising – until I realised the sun had turned the train window into a mirror and she had been watching a sort of silent movie about an anxiety attack.

Whilst I got me some therapy, and support from my super agent, family and friends, I noticed that the place from which I could observe what I was experiencing was where I felt most at home: doing improv. In workshops, I could feel the anxiety rise before I went into the performing space, but I could stop and reflect on it. When I was in scenes, I could apply the improv lessons I had been teaching for so many years to help me ease the anxiety and be in the space. It turned out that, for the last ten years, I had been learning not just the rules of improvisation, but a philosophy for living my life.

Now obviously self-reflective practice isn't possible to do on a stage-stage, where people have paid for you to entertain them. It isn't the place to do extensive inner work, because you need to deliver a Hamilton-inspired number about working in Portsmouth Dockyard and no one has come for you to stop the show and say, 'I'd like to just explore how I am using this Anvil/Granville rhyme to explore my anxiety right now.' So I started to quietly reflect on these things during the workshops I was attending, and then make notes about what exercises helped with which life challenge.

This all led to me creating my course: Improv Your Life. I invite people to come and work on their own lives with me. I help people from all walks of life explore improvisation with a view to implementing it into their day-to-day thinking, doing and being.

I am much better now, thanks for asking. I mention this particular episode so that you know this work is work I have done on myself, as well as with other people. So I understand that life can feel daunting and that being in control seems the obvious solution. That it can feel horrifying to speak your mind, to be seen and to allow your ideas to be voiced. It might seem that being loud and elbowing people out of your way is the only way to get anywhere. Improv shows us this doesn't have to be true. So whatever you are struggling with – being 'too much' or 'not enough' – I promise that improv can provide the space for you to explore what it is you actually need to truly be at one with yourself and the world. It is not turning you into someone else, but simply finding the ways to be the best YOU that you can be.

I often start my workshops with the phrase, 'the most terrifying thing I am going to ask you to do today, is to be yourself', because actually, we don't spend a lot of time really thinking about who that is – beyond our favourite foods and the jobs we do. Some of this is surface work, but it can go as deep as you want it to*.

This book is about me sharing my experiences and the things that have helped me and the people on my course, as well as the hope that some of it rings true for you – that you might try some of these exercises by yourself or with a partner. Or you might be inspired to find an improv class and enjoy being spontaneous and creative, whilst noticing what it throws up for you. Or just take heart that even when you are an expert in something, even if someone looks like they are on top of the world, they can still be struggling. All we are trying to do is convert the struggle into exploration so we don't have to constantly wrestle with ourselves. We can enjoy

---

* That's what she said! Thank you, Michael Scott.

the curiosities that we surprise ourselves, and each other, with daily.

Improv in Life

People often say, 'I can't believe you improvise for a living. I could never do that!', to which I have to reply, 'But you could. You do it all the time!' Humans are brilliant improvisers without even noticing it.

When you go to get the train to work and the train is cancelled, what do you do? You improvise.

'I'll call Hardeep and see if I can get a lift.'

or

'I'll walk – it's only three miles.'

or

'I'll pretend to work from home, but really eat Nutella out of the jar all day in my pants.'

I'm not here to judge how you live your life, just to help you navigate it more fully. Make sure you are enjoying each spoonful of that tasty, tasty chocolate spread.

When you go to the supermarket and there is no lettuce left (true story) so you have to re-plan your meal (even though you were really looking forward to that salad), that is improvising. It is using what is there, in the moment, and making something new.

'No lettuce? Darn. I'll have to have chips instead*.'

---

* Not such a bad outcome, in my opinion.

Improvisation is a mystery to many people because it is so tied up in its identity as a comedy show, rather than a skill in and of itself. So for this book, I would like to use the following definition for improvisation:

Improvisation is the art of using what is available to you in the moment.

Is it the best definition? I don't know – are you the Oxford Dictionary? This definition works for me because the strongest improvisers are the ones who have unlimited access to everything they possess. 'What is available to you' means the people around you, the props on the table and the treasure trove that is yourself. Your thoughts, your words, your responses, your presence in the moment.

The best improvisers are not loud show-offs (not all of them, anyway) – they are curious and interested in the world around them. They want to expand their general knowledge, to be equipped for every scenario. They want to notice every detail, in case it tells them something new or interesting about a character they might play or a scenario they might find themselves in. The general principle of acceptance that runs through improvisation encourages the improviser to notice something rather than rush to judge it.

Improvisers often have varied but deep interests. Amongst my colleagues there is a deep knowledge of jazz, online gaming, alternative lifestyles, pottery, horror, musical theatre, folk music, the Bible, Warhammer and politics. Being interested in the world around you makes you interesting. Curiosity is contagious and fosters the realisation that life is about more than just ourselves. Life is about interacting with the world around us.

To be a top improviser you need, more than anything, to be curious. If you aren't interested in the world or the people around you, then improv is not gonna be an easy place for you. But it can be a way to foster curiosity. And the first thing you need to be curious about is yourself.

Once you get inside yourself, you can get over yourself, and then you can connect to other people. To paraphrase our favourite drag queen:

'If you can't love you, how will you love anyone else?'

Which I always want to expand to:

'If you don't know yourself, how will anyone else?'

And in improv terms:

'If you can't say 'yes' to yourself, why would anyone else?'

Some Basic Improv Terms

Before we get into the nitty gritty of improvising, here are some words that improvisers use all the time to describe their process:

OFFER – This is the thing that a player serves up for another player.

Person A: Hey Dad! I like your haircut.

The offer here is that Person A is speaking to their dad, and that he has had a haircut. Expect all my examples to be this poetic.

COUNTER OFFER – The offer sent back in response to the first offer.

> **Person B:** Thanks, Cindy! I've always admired The
> Beatles. That's why I went for a mop-top.

The counter offer has accepted the original offer of 'haircut' and 'Dad' and built on it, by naming Person A as 'Cindy' (also confirming they are Person B's daughter) and given some detail as to the type of haircut (if you are too young to know what The Beatles looked like, please replace with a more contemporary popstar like Rick Astley).

BLOCK – This is the term for when your offer stops the scene from continuing.

> **Person A:** Hey Dad! Like the new haircut!
> **Person B:** What are you talking about? I am not your dad.
> I am an alien called Fedra and I will destroy you and
> all your robot wives.

A is now confused as **B** has dismissed their original offer of a haircut to make their 'much better' offer – that this is a sci-fi robot fantasy. The scene will awkwardly limp on and no one will be happy until it finishes, and the audience clap out of relief.

PLATFORM – The platform is the basic information gathered for your improvisation scene and is created by the first few offers. It can include information such as your location, your character identities and the activity being pursued. As we add more offers, we will expand the platform, so we need to be sure to remember the details of the world we have created.

REINCORPORATION – The act of bringing something back into the scene that had previously been mentioned before. This is a classic scriptwriting technique to tie stories together:

- A kid dreams of being on a baseball team, and the film ends with them hitting a home run.
- An old lady loses a locket as a young woman, and just as she is about to die, the locket is returned to her.
- A detective finds a cigarette butt at the scene of the crime and thinks nothing of it. Later, when all seems lost, someone mentions they smelt smoke the night of the murder. The detective remembers the cigarette butt and uses the DNA to catch the murderer.

Finally, let us agree three basic rules of improv:

- **Work in Agreement** – You cannot play together if you are aiming for different things.
- **Accept and Build** – Hear what your scene partner(s) say and work with their offers.
- **Have Fun** – Play with your fellow performers and enjoy creating sparks of joy.

What Is My Offer?

By the end of this book you will have thought about:

- How you engage with the words 'yes' and 'no'.
- How to embrace your creativity.
- Failures reimagined as learning points.
- How our wish to be original can prevent us from doing anything at all.
- How the best way for us to be original is to be obvious. Our obvious.
- How long a list needs to be to feel like it's worth the book price.
- Accepting all your wonky and dark bits.
- Accepting other people's wonky and dark bits.
- Being willing to address the wonky and dark bits.
- Speaking your truth.
- How we are never finished as humans and that constant change and adaptation can be daunting.

Also, you will have laughed, cried and bent some pages over to go back to later. And probably spilled some coffee over page 78*.

I have trained lawyers, footballers, IT consultants and actors. I have worked with people suffering from mental health issues and women who have been through the justice system. No matter what their background or occupation, what

---

* Note to editor – let's make page 78 really good.

people responded to was a space to express themselves, to explore their inner world and to find new ways to connect with the people around them.

Let's get started. Let's get seen.

Everyone put your hands in the middle and after three shout, 'Improv Your Life.'

1

2

3

IMPROV YOUR LIFE!

Time to get serious. By getting silly.

A POTTED HISTORY
OF IMPROVISATION

What connects Tina Fey and the ancient Greeks?
Improv!

What connects team building and *Whose Line Is It Anyway?*
Improv!

What connects theatre and breaking the law?
Improv!

Maybe you know some improvisers. Someone might have taken a class, had a workshop at work or be a secret improv geek. Truth is, improv is everywhere. It's like when you think, 'Maybe I'll have pizza for dinner', suddenly pizzas start to appear in your surroundings – adverts, on your phone (because GOOGLE IS LISTENING TO EVERYTHING) and in your mouth (because you gave in). Now you have started reading this book, improvisers will be coming out of the woodwork; appearing at parties, in your break room, at the mother and baby group. 'Oh yes, I did an improv class once,' will start to become something you hear regularly. It is important, therefore, before you are inducted into the great clan of improv, that you know some of what has gone before.

Improv's history is not definitive – it cannot be, because it is a performance style that thrives in its disappearing act. You go on stage and do a show that will never be seen again. This is not an art like painting, where one hundred years down the line someone might still be staring at your creation. It is a practice that encourages us to move along. Improvisation is created in the moment and belongs to that moment. Despite this, I shall attempt to give you a taste of our ephemeral legacy.

Contrary to popular belief, improvisation was not started by *Whose Line Is It Anyway* when it appeared on British TV in 1988 (yes, it was a British show to begin with, then taken to America). In fact, *Whose Line Is It Anyway* started its life on BBC Radio 4, with Clive Anderson as host and regular performers John Sessions and Stephen Fry. It was such a hit on the radio that it was transferred to the telly box. But wait, we are getting ahead of ourselves. If we really want to get into the history of improvisation, we have to go back to ancient Greece.

Improvisation* can be traced all the way back to the ancient Greeks, during a period of performance known as Dorian Mime (mime didn't mean 'silent person in stripy jumper' till much later). As cited in *Improvisation in Drama* by Frost and Yarrow, these little companies of masked actors '. . . specialised in tiny farces on everyday subjects; the stealing of apples, or the arrival of a quack doctor . . . They were also known, most significantly, as *autokabdaloi*, which means "buffoons" and "improvisers".

---

* I have begun with using the full term, 'improvisation', because we are quite far away from 'improv comedy'. The ancient Greeks were not, we don't think, singing hoedowns or playing party quirks.

So, there were tastes of improv in ancient Greece, but it's not until the 16th century, in Italy, that we can more clearly see our improv ancestors. This was known as a theatre form called commedia dell'arte – the Italian masked character plays that went from town to town. Each performer would know their character and the scenario, but wouldn't have much more than some stock phrases, which they would weave amongst improvised dialogue. This new, on-the-spot dialogue would bring in local information from the very town the performance was in, such as you might find a stand-up comic in Oxford making jokes about the one-way system. There was a spontaneity, an observational wit about commedia dell'arte that excited the crowd.

Despite this propensity to add spontaneous dialogue, it is not until the 1950s and 60s that we get fully improvised shows advertised as such. One of the most influential of these spaces was The Second City in Chicago, which opened in 1959. They believed that improvisation (previously only used to devise theatre and sketches) was good enough to be seen in its immediate form. This was the beginning of what we now know as 'improv comedy' (sometimes in the UK this is called American-style improv and usually means super fast and super funny). The Second City became the birthplace of hundreds of comic performers (Tina Fey, Bill Murray, Mike Myers to name but a tiny few) and inspired many other American improv troupes (The Groundlings, Upright Citizens Brigade, Improv Olympic), as the actors learned how to think fast on their feet, be hilarious and create narrative pieces to entertain the crowd. What a legacy.

The Second City's work was inspired by and used the work of one of improv's mothers, Viola Spolin. Viola was working as a drama teacher in the 1930s, during which time she became fascinated by the idea of using play as a way to teach children drama. The games she developed allowed the player to tap into their intuition and become free to respond 'in the moment'. This meant that in a dramatic scene, the performer would respond intuitively, rather than mechanically.

This was revolutionary for acting technique. It is hard to imagine that now, with TV being all about close, intimate acting based in naturalism. However, Viola was influenced by the work of Konstantin Stanislavski and Anton Chekov – two theatre practitioners who were starting the naturalistic acting revolution. Acting focused less on emotional truth back then and more on showing emotion through fixed gestures and loud, booming voices. At the time, most acting was what we call 'melodramatic'. Stanislavski and Chekov's wish was to have actors connected to the text and the other actors in the scene. It took a concerted effort to move from 'show and tell' acting to 'feel and reveal'.

So, improv comedy was already cooking in public in the US before we had any official improvisation theatre in the UK. Why? Do the Brits love scripts that much? No (in fact, if you ask most improvisers why they like improv, it's because they don't have to learn any lines*). It was because we still had theatre censorship until 1968, meaning the Lord Chamberlain

---

* Improvisation has actually made it almost impossible for me to learn lines anymore, because I make them up so much. My memory doesn't think holding onto words is important. I rarely say a written line as written. It is not a popular trait when doing someone else's play. However, I will never not know what to say on stage – I just might not say what you wanted me to.

(sounds like a fool already, doesn't he?) went through any play for public performance and deemed whether it should be allowed on stage; cutting or changing lines and even stage directions to make them morally acceptable. Improvisation was thought dangerous, because there was no way the authorities could know what was going to be said, so how could they control what the people would hear? This meant it was forbidden by the authorities for any divergence by a theatre company from the script that had been permitted by the censors.

This doesn't mean improvisation didn't happen. Joan Littlewood was a revolutionary theatre director who created Theatre Workshop, a band of theatre folk who made work that reflected the political time they were working in. Theatre Workshop productions were devised (improvising in the rehearsal room but with a fixed show at the end of the process), however, Joan was prosecuted *twice* for allowing her actors to improvise during shows. Imagine that – being hauled up before a judge because you allowed people to respond in the moment. See? Improvisation is dangerous. Because we might say what we mean, or think, or feel. We might intuit what the audience is thinking and feeling. We might inspire a crowd to go forth and speak their mind. Improvisation might be the revolution. And so, it was illegal. Viva la improvisation!

Around the same time, we're talking mid-60s, Keith Johnstone was working with actors at the Royal Court Theatre, London. He noticed they were not able to create realistic scenes, because they were too busy acting. So Keith started inventing games in which the actors might create dynamic and nuanced relationships with each other and be able to stay in the moment rather than stand in the space as two-dimensional characters that were trying to think up clever things to say.

Despite not having an actual aim for serious theatre with these exercises, hilarity ensued. The actors and Keith kept laughing. The humour that was generated by these situations and games was astounding. Keith wanted to see what happened in front of an audience – were the actors just laughing at each other or was this really funny to an outsider? To get around that pesky Lord Chamberlain, Keith started putting on 'live comedy-writing workshops' that the Lord Chamberlain didn't get involved with because they weren't officially 'performances'. These not-really-shows-but-really-were shows had packed audiences, and became a massive hit.

When theatre censorship was abolished in 1968, Keith and his players were able to improvise freely. These workshops eventually transformed into The Theatre Machine: a group of actors performing totally improvised performances in the UK and around Europe – spreading the word that improvisation, as a show in itself, had arrived.

There is no doubt that Theatre Machine was the beginning of the UK improv revolution. Improv shows started popping up all over, with an explosion in London in the 1980s. Theatres like Gate Theatre in Notting Hill, The Tricycle Theatre (now known as The Kiln Theatre) in Kilburn and The Donmar Warehouse in Covent Garden all ran improvised performances alongside their scripted shows.

The longest-running British improv troupe to this very day* is the Comedy Store Players, who emerged in 1985 when Mike Myers (yes, Austin Powers himself) and Kit Hollerbach taught their friends Neil Mullarky, Dave Cohen and Paul Merton a couple of improv games. Until the Great Lockdown of 2020, they had played The Comedy Store on Wednesdays and Sundays every week, though the line-up has changed a little (but not much). Josie Lawrence and Richard Vranch joined in 1986, followed by Lee Simpson and (for a while) Sandi Toksvig in 1987.

Improvisation wasn't just happening in comedy clubs, however. It was also being used as a tool for community theatre – a way to help people find and speak their truth. Devising became a common practice for theatre groups, from Theatre of Black Women – who created work exploring the experience of being Black in Britain in the 1980s – to Theatre de Complicité (now known simply as Complicité) – who combined physical theatre with text and music to create beautiful, mind-boggling pieces that expanded and explored the imagination. Companies like Fluxx were moved by how powerful improvisation could be harnessed as a tool for change, and took improvisation into places like prisons as a way to develop communication skills and devise theatrical pieces that told the inmates' stories. This type of work continues to this day with companies such as Cardboard Citizens, who create theatre with members of the homeless community, and The

---

* Unless you are reading this book in a retro cool way in 2085, in which case I am sorry to say, we are all dead.

Comedy School, who use improv workshops to promote mental health.

Since the beginning of UK improv at the Royal Court, there have been many companies growing and exploring improvisation. We have had theatrical excellence in *Austentatious*, *Improbable* and The Showstoppers. We have comedy excellence, community building and teaching from our improv schools including Hoopla, The Nursery, The Suggestibles, Bristol Improv Theatre and The Free Association. On TV, improvisation has been used as a tool in shows such as *Borderline* (Channel 5) and *The Thick of It* (BBC). On Netflix, *Middleditch & Schwartz* have earned the title of the first long-form, completely improvised show to be broadcast in its simplest form. Improvisers such as Amy Poehler, Tina Fey and Will Ferrell have taken Hollywood by storm, and there will be more. There is no doubt that the 21st century is an exciting time for improv.

You now know about two per cent of the history of improvisation. That will do for now. For it is time to learn.

Failure Oath

Before every workshop, I ask my students to take this oath, to remind them that failure is part of the process. Whether we are improvising a scene, learning how to drive or trying not to lose our temper with a colleague, we often don't get it right first time. And that is OK.

Please read the following out loud –
even if you are on a train.
Especially if you are on a train.

I (insert name) promise

to fail beautifully,

courageously

and with curiosity

as I go on this journey

with Pippa at my side (or in my ear).

(shouted) YES PLEASE THANK YOU

LET'S BE HAVING YOU!

WHO ARE YOU?

WHAT ARE YOU DOING?

How did it feel being asked those three questions, and seeing them typed out all big and direct? Those three questions (often shortened to 'Who What Where') are used in improvisation to ground our scenes in their reality, and so I would like to offer them up to you as a tool for grounding yourself in situations where you are unfamiliar with what is going on or to clarify a situation you are about to enter.

Direct questions can feel almost aggressive; they can turn us instantly into a rabbit in headlights. Is there a correct answer? Of all the possible direct questions, 'Who are you?' may be the most terrifying, triggering an existential crisis in the majority of us. People spend years in therapy trying to discover their true self and investigating all the different versions of themselves. *Les Misérables* features the epic song, 'Who Am I?', where Jean Valjean considers whether he is a good citizen or still a number in the prison system. That song stirs the audience every time, as it conjures a recognition within each of us – that deep wish to know our place in the world. To feel a sense of belonging to a community and know our role within it. A feeling of purpose.

Well, don't worry, we ain't going to be dealing with that vast question right this minute. For the purposes of this section, rather than 'Who Are You?' I would like us to think of the slightly extended version: 'Who Are You *in this Moment?*'

It's possible that these questions feel affronting because they are usually only asked in situations when we feel we are in trouble. Security guards might shout them as you accidentally take a shortcut across private property. If you have ever been to America, passport control often ask these questions so forcefully you start to wonder if perhaps you *are* actually a drug mule and you *did* book that holiday to Dollywood as a cover. Standing there, nervous, as they ask in an accusatory tone: 'Who are you? Where are you going? What are you doing in my country?' Due to assumptions about someone's Who What Where, some people are asked these questions more than others. It is known that Black people are almost 10 times more likely to be stopped and searched by police in the UK than white people due to racial profiling. Asian people are 11 times more likely to be questioned at UK borders than white people. Who What Where, in this instance, isn't just affronting, but exhausting and distressing. Knowing who you are, where you are and what you are doing should be something that is freeing rather than needed as a defence. If this has been your experience, I hope that this chapter will allow you a space for Who What Where to be liberating – embracing the Who What Where to ground us in the moment.

A Who What Where Fail

I remember going to a pantomime audition in Wolverhampton in 2005. It was the beginning of my career, so I would go to any audition that would take me (I hadn't been to drama school proper, so I had to find my way by turning up to rooms and selling my wares, like a dodgy wheeler-dealer specialising in Victoria Wood sketches).

The audition was for a Theatre in Education (TIE) company, which generally means the show goes into schools or residential homes. You play multiple parts and do workshops after with kids or elderly folks. That's the kind of work that suits my personality (good at multi-tasking, find people amusing, lots of biscuits in the staff room), so I was feeling pretty confident that I could get this job. The company informed me that at the audition, I would have to perform a monologue and a song. Songs I can learn like that *clicks fingers*. I still remember most of the songs from my childhood – especially theme tunes from the 80s and 90s*.

A monologue is different, however. They take me ages to learn. I know this about myself. Did I make sure I put the time aside to learn it over those six weeks before the audition? Did I ask a friend to help me rehearse it one afternoon so I could be word perfect? Nope. Instead of preparing it over a few days, I left it right to the last minute. Then, as if I wasn't self-sabotaging enough, I tried to learn it sat at the back of a Megabus, back when the Megabus was exactly that – a mega bus. An old double-decker bus, haring up the M40. I don't know what I was doing – I get travel sick from trying to read maps, let alone fiercely studying a pirate monologue. Needless to say, the learning was not a success. I was about to go and do a half-learnt monologue in front of 30 actors†, all hungry for the part

---

* A much-underrated skill, in my opinion. If you see me in person, ask me if I remember the Riesen 'chocolate chew' jingle . . .

† One of the hardest experiences of being an actor is the group audition. A room of people who are all desperate for a job but having to be super generous and supportive to each other, to show that you can work in a team. You stand there, delivering your monologue, knowing that at least 90 per cent of those beaming faces are thinking, 'I could do better than that'. If you can get through this, you can get through anything.

of Fairy Godmother/Prince/Rat 3. In the last few moments before the audition was due to start, I was desperately trying to learn the text. Stood in this ill-lit corridor of some strange industrial building I had hauled myself to from London, the words were bouncing back off my head to the page, when suddenly a tiny man in platform shoes appeared.

'Who are you?' he said.

I looked up. It was the director.

Bollocks.

'Pippa Evans.'

'And what are you doing?' he said, smoothing his brown flares*.

'Just practising my monologue,' I ventured, hiding the piece of paper behind my back.

'Well, if you don't know it now, you never will,' he said. 'Come on. We're getting started.'

I walked in and sat amongst the throng of preening actors and actresses, all with our fake smiles plastered on.

'Good luck, everyone,' said the most attractive woman I have ever seen. She looked at me with a glint in her eye that said: 'You've got no chance, babes.' And she was right.

The Director decided to call me up to perform my monologue first. Perhaps he was being kind and letting me get it out of the way, but I felt like a lamb being led to the slaughter. I stumbled and stalled through my swashbuckling pirate speech. I don't know if you are familiar with pirates, but they

---

* No word of a lie – the company had been going since the early 70s and this guy had no intention of moving forward from those glory days.

aren't generally portrayed as tripping over their words whilst going red in the face. It was prettttty awkward. As I went to sit down, I got one of those pity rounds of applause. You know, when everyone is just relieved that they aren't you. The director looked at the rest of the room, and then looked at me, and said, 'It's a shame, isn't it? When we let ourselves down.' I wanted to run straight out the door but instead I had to sit back down in the group and listen to 29 other monologues, followed by the Director telling anecdotes from his 35 years in theatre. It was a long three hours, especially when I knew I hadn't got the job.

I rode the Megabus back to London sat next to a guy eating a tube of sour cream and chive Pringles. As I breathed in his savoury stench, I thought about what I'd just done. Why had I gone all the way to Wolverhampton for an audition I hadn't prepared for? What was I doing? Acting is a highly competitive world, and vicious in many ways – so why had I gone in there not having done the work that would ensure I represented myself well? Here I was, Pippa Evans, feeling annoyed at myself for doing something I thought I wanted to do (become an actor), but not committing to it. Lazy and possibly even arrogant. Why did this Pippa show up?

Doing the Groundwork

The simple answer is, I hadn't taken the time to consider the Who What Where of this activity. Who did I need to be in order to get this job? What did I need to do? Where was probably the only bit I sorted out, by buying my Megabus ticket. In any improvisation scene, if there is a sense that something isn't quite right, it is usually because one of these factors isn't in place. For my audition, I hadn't thought about the qualities I needed to display, number one being the ability to learn and perform my lines. I needed to turn up with calm, self-assured Pippa rather than frantic, underprepared Pippa. I could have figured out my Who by thinking: 'Who are they looking for?' Answer: Reliable actors who can cope in any situation*.

Thinking about it now, I hadn't thought about my What either. What was I doing? I was going to get a job. I was going to represent myself to a room full of people. I was going to show off my performance skills. If I'd thought about that in advance, perhaps I would have recognised the work I needed to put in before I got in the audition room. It is possible that thinking about the What was too overwhelming for me, so I was subconsciously making sure I didn't have all the variables in place. That way my rejection would not be about my acting skills, but about my lack of prep. I would be able to say, 'If I'd learnt the monologue, I would have got it.' Which is a lot less painful than saying, 'I wasn't what they were looking for.'

––––––––––––––––––

* I went on to do a couple of TIE projects with other companies and you literally need to have the adaptability of Japanese knotweed. You turn up with the show to some corner of the land and you put it on, in whatever space is available. Corners of rooms, big auditoriums, corridors. I am pretty sure the phrase, 'The show must go on!' comes not from the West End but rather the many educational shows about bullying or recycling turning up to schools who say, 'Oh – is it today?'

Who What Where – Three-Line Initiation

Exploring Who What and Where is essential in improv training as a way to indoctrinate the idea of parameters needed for a scene within which the performers flourish. It is this information which is fundamental to creating the platform that the scene is built on. I was introduced to the three-line initiation exercise by a Canadian improviser called David Shore. In David's version, we would stand in pairs and have to – in a short, three-line exchange between us – say who we were, where we were, and what we were doing. It looked like this:

> **Person 1:** And half a pound of sausages, my good fellow!
> **Person 2:** Half a pound, Mrs Flanigan? That's going to be quite the feast!
> **Person 1:** Yes, Mr Leary. And if it's going to be a feast, we need the best sausages in town*!

WHO – Shopkeeper and customer (Mr Leary and Mrs Flanigan)
WHAT – Buying/selling sausages
WHERE – Butcher's/grocer's shop

With all three ingredients, it is super clear where the scene is set, and easy for us to visualise the world. Perhaps you imagined what the characters looked like. Maybe you could see those sausages. We are no longer just some improvisers in

---

* A lot of my scenes seem to be set in 1950s Britain.

a room above a pub. Now we have created a rich, new world to explore.

When people first try this exercise, it doesn't tend to roll off the tongue. Instead, it is usual for the delivery to be incredibly clunky:

> **Person 1:** Hello . . . Mum! So excited to be in the lounge of our house that we live in . . . today!
>
> **Person 2:** Hello daughter to whom I am Mum! I love being in the lounge on your . . . birthday!
>
> **Person 1:** Is that cake all for me, here in the lounge, on my birthday, Mum?

WHO – Mother and daughter
WHAT – Celebrating birthday with cake
WHERE – In their lounge

From this exchange, we have got all the information we need. Although the dialogue is delivered as if by children in a nativity play, nervous they might forget that the baby is called Jesus, the point of the exercise isn't to create a brilliant performance, but rather to practise making strong statements about what is going on. This is excellent practise for checking in on your aim and purpose in the scene, and being clear with each other about the agreed reality of the situation you are in.

Like most improvisation, we get the clearest learning point when we get it wrong. When we play this exercise with only vague offers, we can immediately see what trouble looks like:

Person 1: Hi. You here for the thing?
Person 2: Yeah. You?
Person 1: Yes. Heard a lot about it.

Three lines and we know nothing apart from the fact that there is a 'thing'*. What is going on here? No clarity of purpose or statements. The scene is stalling – it is going nowhere. It is an awkward date that no one wanted to be invited to. If we were in a class, I would ask, 'What do we know?' and the two improvisers would giggle and say, 'There is a "thing"'. And then we'd talk about why we didn't just name the thing. It can be anything, and yet we didn't want to commit to what it was, in case it wasn't that after all.

I am drawn to a parallel here with the work of philosopher Ivan Illich, who suggested that our unrest as humans comes from too much choice. Illich thought that the only way for humans to enjoy life was to give some of that choice up. When we reduce our choices, paradoxically, we are more free. Think how much easier it is to choose your clothes from a suitcase than a wardrobe, which route to take in the car when there are only two options, instead of fourteen. Until you commit to something, you cannot enjoy it, and if there are too many

---

*The only way this would work in the context of a performance is if it were performed by fantastic actors who can make subtext bleed out of every orifice. Great performers can get away with doing nothing, because it is never nothing – the intention is always there, in their very being. But a lot of the time, we are not great actors. We are awkward improvisers not wanting to commit to a Who What Where in case the audience thinks it sucks. And so, in our worrying that it will suck, we manifest that it does.

choices, that commitment becomes harder to achieve. It's the same in improv – we find it hard to make the choice of the setting when the options are so huge, but will ultimately find satisfaction by committing to one idea and exploring it, instead of floundering amongst a thousand.

Demanding Our Who What Where

When I was first introduced to this exercise, it amazed me how hard it was to instantly accept a fictional situation that has been given to you; to set the tracks down according to your instinct when you weren't consulted in the first instance.

More surprising, though, is how hard it is to tell the person opposite you what *you* think the scene should be. When you have to make that first demand of Where, or Who or What. Students stall or look to me for advice or give their offer with a sense of apology, like they have already decided it isn't a very good one. It is hard for us to take charge of situations and lay down some of the boundaries and realities that we want for ourselves, even if it's just one or two.

Imagine going to a job interview. A space where we need to express our Who What Where in very specific parameters. This is a very literal use of Who What Where – the interviewer will no doubt ask us about who we are, what we are doing in life and where we are currently working. How often have we tried to guess what the person sat opposite us wants us to say, rather than embody what we think we can offer them? How often have we turned up, underprepared, not knowing how we want to present ourselves today, because we weren't quite sure what they wanted and perhaps we didn't believe we had it in us. Or perhaps, even, we didn't really want the job. We were there because we thought we wanted a change, or someone had told us we were 'really well suited' to the role. Whatever the reason, we hadn't done enough work to know our Who What and Where. If we go back to my audition, I didn't have my Who What Where* in order. I turned up as Pippa the nervous wreck instead of Pippa the prepared, reliable, pretty good actor. Where was I? I was all over the place.

Let's look at an example of a job interview where we haven't thought about our Who What Where. This is going to be exaggerated, but it will give you a sense of how to explore Who What Where in a formal situation.

Our candidate is going for the role of manager at their local Sainsbury's.

Interviewer: Tell me, what made you apply for this job?
Interviewee: Ummm, well, I like shopping at Sainsbury's
    and I do a lot of shopping (awkward laugh at own
    joke) and I think I would make a great manager.
Interviewer: What would make you a great manager?
Interviewee: Well, I have three children, so I can make
    people do what they don't want to do! (More
    awkward laughing) Also, I have been a manager
    before and I was pretty good at that. And I live down
    the road, so I won't be late to work. Although they say
    the late ones are always the ones who live closest.

---

* I love how much this sounds like a euphemism.

Interviewer: Do they? How interesting. So where would
you like to be in five years' time?

Interviewee: I don't know, Jamaica? It's warm there!
Joking, no. I would love to be a more senior manager.
Is there a word for that?

Interviewer: Area manager, perhaps?

Interviewee: Manager-manager would be more fun.

Interviewer: Yes. Yes, it would. Well . . . thank you very
much for coming in.

Interviewee: (With sense that it hasn't gone as well as it
could have done) Orange is my favourite colour!

Interviewer: Sorry?

Interviewee: Your bags. And your logo. They are all
orange. (Pause) I like orange*.

Interviewer: We'll let you know.

Oh, that was so painful to type. The squirming and the joking
are all there because the solid foundations of Who What
Where weren't in place, creating a discomfort for the two
folks in the interview. Without having prepared the Who What
Where, our interviewee has not been able to present themselves in the light they would like to be seen. Let's give them
another chance.

Interviewer: Tell me, what made you apply for this job?

Interviewee: Well, I have worked in retail for the last ten
years and I think I'd like a bit more responsibility. I
am good at organising people and tend to get projects

---

* This is genuinely why I shop at Sainsbury's.

finished, so management feels like a good next step for me.

Interviewer: What makes you feel you could be a manager?

Interviewee: In my last job, I was in charge of the lower floor of Boots, Hampton Road. That meant making sure there were enough people on the tills and stocking shelves, taking their breaks. I was managing my area and I did it well.

Interviewer: You're moving on from one job, so where would you like to be in five years' time?

Interviewee: I am looking for some stability. So ideally, I would be continuing to work at manager level or above with the Sainsbury's group.

Interviewer: Why with Sainsbury's?

Interviewee: I think you treat your customers and employees well. And I love the colour orange.

Interviewer: Great to meet you, Interviewee. You'll be hearing from us soon.

What a much more comfortable interview to read. We can see that our interviewee has pushed her managerial qualities to the front of her mind, that the role she needs to play here is 'kickass candidate for managerial position' – it is clear that she is confident in her abilities and has considered all the basic questions likely to come up in a job interview. The 'orange' joke at the end brings forward an element of her fun qualities without undermining her qualifications. This woman is a serious contender and will most likely be enjoying her 20 per cent employee discount soon enough.

When we consider our Who What Where in specific situations, we can start to really commit to how we want to be in a meeting, at a party or any situation where we might want to show up fully.

A Note on the Who*

When people first start improvising scenes, the student considers the Who to be fixed by just using a name. 'Hello, Kwame, how are you?' they might say. The other improviser has been provided with a name, but that is hugely limited information. What does a name tell us? 'That which we call a rose / By any other name would smell as sweet,' Shakespeare says. Logic follows then, that names are mainly sorting labels, differentiating Kwame from Barbara, and stopping you from just yelling, 'Hey, you!' across a room when you want someone's attention.

For the character to become tangible, we need to know the role they are holding during this scene. We have so many different roles in our lives. Those that we are born into (e.g. human, sister, daughter) and those we take on (e.g. partner, carer, employee). What role is the character in at this moment in the scene? Are they a shopkeeper serving their customer? Are they a parent scolding their child? It is the relationship they hold to the other character whilst in this role that gives a fuller picture of the Who.

---

* Not the band.

For example, they are a window cleaner, but they are working with their dad. So, in this moment, they are a son and a window cleaner. Move the same character to a pub with his friends and suddenly he is a friend more than he is a son. Now we can see that our roles shift as to Where we are, Who we are with and What we are doing with those people. Which means that if we haven't kept an eye on our Who What Where, we might not be showing up with the right costume on.

In *The Roles We Play*, a photographic project created with Eva Sajovic and ATD Fourth World*, people living in poverty in the UK were given the chance to choose the best way of describing their role in life, which would be put next to their photo in a collection of images from some of the UK's benefit claimants. They chose the roles that they play in their community, rather than the label they had been given by society. Being described as a 'philosopher' or 'freedom fighter' gave them the opportunity to be portrayed, as one participant described, 'in a decent light, rather than as one of these thieving scumbags on benefits ... it allowed me to take control of my public perception.'

By giving people the chance to choose their Who, rather than having it put upon them, they were able to feel empowered and it changed not only the way society saw them, but how they saw themselves.

---

* All Together in Dignity Fourth World is an international charity working to eradicate poverty through giving those affected a voice to speak their truth.

The Long Game of Who What Where

Take a moment to think about the world you live in.

Who are you in that?

Now ...

Who do you want to be?

What do you want to be doing?

Where do you want to be?

These are big questions that we need to keep coming back to because the answers will and do change over time. *Who* we want to be at 15 is probably quite different to who we want to be at 40. Perhaps your ambition as a teen was to hold a specific job like a doctor or TV presenter and now it is more of a state of being that is more values-based; wanting to be kind, generous, fierce or all the above. We can reflect on Who we are *now* and use that to decide Who we might like to develop into, be that based in vocation or virtues*.

What do you want to be doing is a question about action. What action are you partaking in right now? If you want to change your job from hairdresser to psychiatrist, what steps are you taking to make that happen? If you want to change the government's policies around climate change, how can you take action to make that happen?

---

* Virtues are the essence of our character, things like courage, compassion, understanding. They are characteristics which grow with us as we age rather than being achievements we can tick off.

Where do you want to be might refer to a physical place ('I want to be living in Stoke-on-Trent'), or it might be a position in a pre-existing hierarchy ('I want to have made it to management') or stage of life ('I want to be having my second child').

Our Who What Where is a constantly adapting idea when we are thinking about living out our entire lives. Use the questions to help you make decisions on actions you need to take for long-term change.

If we keep checking in on our Who What Where, we can start to feel less anxious about the day-to-day achievements and milestones that society puts on us, because we gain a deeper insight into our bigger-picture needs and desires. If I were to get a tattoo, it would be three Ws on my arm, to remind me to ground myself in Who What Where when I find myself getting anxious. Unfortunately, it would look like I was turning my arm into a website.

Use Who What Where for immediate check-ins with yourself. Before an important meeting, tell yourself who you are, where you are and what you want from this situation. When catching up with a friend who has been hurtful to you, check in with who you want them to see, where you are in your relationship and what you want to do, moving forward. When considering the next milestone in your life – moving house, changing career, getting married or getting divorced – use Who What Where to think about the bigger picture. Who do you want to be able to be? What do you want from this new chapter? Where do you want it to take you?

Who are you? · Where are you? · What are you doing?

Exercise Corner

It's time for you to have a go at the three-line initiation exercise.

SOLO

Write down Who What Where on a piece of paper like this:

Who

What

Where

Try to define yourself in these terms for yourself right now. This moment as you are reading this book. Then do the same but for you 10 years ago. Who were you then? This can be as literal or poetic as you like. For instance:

Who: A stand-up.

What: Honing my skills.

Where: The comedy circuit in London.

or

Who: An ambitious dreamer.

What: Trying to ride the waves.

Where: The sea of showbiz.

See how many of these definitions of yourself you can discover. You might find you are an 'ambitious dreamer' in one and a 'hopeless romantic' in the other. You can see how many roles you have played in your life and reflect on how they have served you. Do you miss any of them? Have you forgotten some of them? When you think you have exhausted your list, push to find one more. It is at this point that we often surprise ourselves with what we discover.

IN A PAIR

In each chapter, I offer an exercise you can do with another person, so invite your friend, your sibling or your partner to join you.

Creating Platforms

Stand opposite each other, and within three lines of dialogue between you, try to express:

Who you are (character defined by relationship/job/name).
What you are doing (activity, reason for being there).
Where you are (physical space, geographical space).

See how many characters you can create. Invent names for them (my characters are often called Peter – enjoy discovering your default names), and give as much detail as you can. Make sure you accept every detail given back to you by your second character.

By practising Who What Where on imaginary scenarios, we enable ourselves to explore our real-life scenarios more easily, knowing we have this language to hand. It also enables us to explore imaginary futures for ourselves. Imagine some Who What Where scenarios that you might like to embrace in the years to come. Answer those questions I asked earlier:

Who do you want to be?
What do you want to be?
Where do you want to be?

Be as abstract or ambitious as you wish – we're playing with your future, not deciding it.

Through play, the serious work can be done.

Looking and Listening

People often come up to me at the end of an improv show and say: 'WOW! That was amazing. I just don't know how you did that!' and then they ask for all the secrets.

'What are your SECRETS?' they whisper, conspiratorially.

'You can tell me – I won't tell anyone.'

They glance to the side, to see if anyone else is listening.

'Do you talk to each other in the wings?'

'Do you have secret hand codes?'

'Do you wear earpieces, and someone tells you what to say?'

The answer to all these questions is, 'No'.

'What we do, I am sorry to tell you, is we look, listen and respond.' I say. And most often, this person will wink and reply, 'Alright. OK. Sure – if you don't want to tell me, that's fine.'

And they go on their merry way, thinking that improv pays enough for us to create mini-autocue contact lenses that we stick in our eyes before every show.

But it really is as simple as I tell them.

Look. Listen. Respond.

How many times do you think you are listening when you are actually thinking about what you want to have for dinner? How many times do you think you are looking at someone but actually you are staring into space?

When you are fully present with someone – looking at everything in front of you and listening to everything that is being said – you have so much information, that what you want to do next – what you need to do next – becomes so clear. So intuitive. Because you are simply responding to what you have seen and heard. But in a world of smartphones and headphones, adverts and bright signs, apps for everything and overstimulation for our little hunter-gatherer brains, looking and listening becomes incredibly difficult. Because we suddenly see an advert for a McFlurry® and think, 'Shall I have a McFlurry®?' And then your friend says, 'Do you agree?' and you say, 'Go for it!' because you didn't hear what they said before, but they are looking hopeful and so you don't want to tell them you were thinking about a McFlurry® instead of listening to them. And then you realise that you've just told them you think they should ask out that idiot from PC World.

When we are improvising, it becomes really obvious when we haven't been listening. We come in with an offer that doesn't match what has been going on.

> **Person A:** And that is why we are never moving to Dorset, Dawn.
>
> **Person B:** Sorry? Oh yes, Devon is horrible, isn't it.

In a show, this will be a hilarious, awkward moment for the audience. In life, we are stung by being caught not listening or mishearing and our partner smarts us from not having our full attention.

A friend of mine was talking to a colleague at work about her recent holiday. My friend said, 'We went to Spain and when we got back, my dog had died', to which her colleague replied, 'I've been to Spain.'

This isn't not listening, it is not listening fully. To the end. So often we start forming our answer before the sentence is finished. We are excited by what has been said, so we start to formulate our response, missing the last point, and then, when we excitedly say what we think is conversation gold, it lands flat because we missed the most important bit of information.

And whatever you do, don't forget to listen with your whole body* as well as your colleague's body. Their voice, their physical offers, their face. All of these things add to the meaning of what is being said.

Imagine someone saying the line, 'Have you seen Tez?'

Now imagine someone saying the line whilst smoking a cigar in an armchair.

Now imagine someone saying it curled up, crying on the sofa.

Now imagine someone saying it holding a birthday cake, looking excited.

Same words, many different meanings. Words are not all we need to listen to.

---

* Back up a minute. What? Yes – we give off so many signals that our bodies might 'hear' something that our ears can't. Like when you know someone is watching you for no reason other than your body felt it. Or you sense something good is about to happen when someone comes in the room with 'I've got a surprise for you' energy. Or when your tummy tells you that you don't think this nativity play is going to be ten minutes long, as advertised, and you are right. You sense that something doesn't add up, but you can't always explain it. That is listening with your body. More on this later.

We are not and never will be perfect at listening. Even with all my training, I just asked my husband the same question four times because I stopped listening to the answer. I started thinking about a funny song I might write. But I noticed – and that, my friends, is half the battle.

Improv is a unique training because it asks you to respond to everything as brand new, to not guess what is wanted but to respond in the moment. The only way to do this is to really look and really listen before you make the next offer. The same is true of any human interaction. Pay attention to what is being offered to you.

Breathe it all in and the responses will flow.

Exercise Corner

SOLO

Watch a video on YouTube – anything. Could be a make-up tutorial, the news, a flat-earther conspiracy experiment – whatever floats your boat. Watch the video and take note of every time your attention drifts from what they are saying. Stop the video halfway through and try to relay the information in the video back to yourself, out loud. It is amazing how much we trick ourselves into the idea that we are listening because we are in the physical position of listening, when actually we are planning our next album with Ringo Starr*.

IN A PAIR

One person says a sentence. Doesn't matter what it is, as long as it is a statement, rather than a question. The next person will use a word or phrase from that sentence to keep connected to what was said before. This continues until the conversation feels finished. For example:

Person A: There is a butterfly at the window again.
Person B: Butterflies love windows. Apparently they
        mistake them for very clean air.

---

* He doesn't know it yet, but we have a bestseller on our hands when he finally answers those Instagram messages I've been sending him.

Person A: <u>Very clean air</u>? I find that hard to believe.

Person B: <u>Believe</u> whatever you like – I read it in a magazine so it must be true.

Person A: What <u>magazine</u>?

Person B: *Gardeners' World*, that's what <u>magazine</u>!

This exercise keeps the participants connected as they really listen to what words they might borrow and also which word was borrowed from them. It helps you to develop your listening techniques and notice where the train of thought is going. The characters are on the same page, but still speaking their own minds, creating their own responses*.

---

* N.B. This is not to be used in a normal situation. You will seem like you have been on a course for how to talk to people. But it CAN be very useful if you have lost concentration mid-conversation as a way to hook back into the flow. Use it sparingly.

TAKE UP SPACE

When I was a kid, I learnt the violin*. On a Saturday, I would go down to my primary school which had been transformed into a hub for music learning. Children had group instrument lessons, which meant lots of kids learning their instrument at the same time – you can imagine the cacophony pouring down the corridors as we heard guitars, drums and flutes being played en masse by enthusiastic kittens. I was ten years old and a new term was starting. Ten being the arrival into double digits, I was deemed old enough to walk to class all by myself. The school was not far from my house, but it felt very grown up. I was in charge of myself for the first time. Arriving at the reception area ('reception area' meaning 'harassed lady surrounded by registers, lists and classroom numbers, sitting in a chair designed for a primary school student'), I was told to go to Room 12 and pointed up the corridor to Miss Leveson's class. I didn't know Miss Leveson – this was a new teacher. And the classrooms during the week were known by colours, not numbers. I didn't know what 'Room 12' meant. But I didn't ask because

---

* My parents liked to torture themselves, clearly. Or perhaps the neighbours . . .

I was grown up now and grown-ups don't need directions. So I wandered off, gingerly, in the direction the receptionist had pointed.

I could feel a panic start to rise in my throat as I began to doubt which room I was supposed to be in. The door I arrived at didn't have a number, so I wasn't sure that the door I was standing outside was the right door. I could hear violins being played, so there was a big clue there, but something bigger than self-belief arrived and took over my being: fear of looking like an idiot. I knew I should just go in and ask if this was Miss Leveson's class, but I was too worried that I would be wrong and get in trouble for interrupting the lesson, or that the other kids would laugh at me. I stood outside the door and waited, hoping someone would come out of the classroom and say, 'Oh – is that you, Pippa Evans? We've all been waiting for you – come on in!' And then I would go in and everyone would cheer. 'Pippa is here! Pippa is here! Play your violin, Pippa! Play!*'

But they didn't.

Instead, I shrunk into the wall, standing in the corridor for 45 minutes, torn between going into the room or running home, until finally the class ended and the other kids came out.

One of the students stopped and said, 'Are you Pippa?' and relieved to have been acknowledged, I said, 'Yes!'

'You've just missed your violin lesson. Why didn't you come in?' Leaving the question in the air, she flounced off

---

* This is how I wish most people greeted me. One day . . .

with her new classmates for an orange squash and a Nice biscuit*.

I felt like such a weirdo. And now I had to go home and explain to my mum that I had missed my class, which she couldn't understand.

'Why didn't you just go in?' Mum also asked, bemused.

I thought for a bit and then said, 'I was worried everyone would look at me when I opened the door and then I worried I would be in the wrong room and they would all laugh and my face would go red. So I just waited for someone to tell me what to do.'

'Oh darling,' my mum said, making lunch, 'That is a lot of things to worry about at once.'

And she was right. All because I didn't want to take up any space.

So often, when we are in a world or a room or a situation where we might have to take up some space or have attention directed towards us, where we might stand out, an anxiety arises that we are going to take that space – that opportunity – and make a fool of ourselves. It can be anything from asking for directions to giving a keynote speech. We create a mind montage of all the things that could go wrong in the next few minutes, meaning we freeze in that moment. We deliberate over what we could do and how that choice might pan out

---

* Literally a Nice biscuit. The ones that said 'NICE' on them. The music school must have had a deal with the Nice biscuit company because no one chooses Nice biscuits. They are a 'last to the biscuit tin' biscuit – eaten only by those who were not fast enough to get the Jaffa Cakes.

and then, because we were not present in the moment, the actual moment disappears. Have you ever not asked a question because people would look at you? Have you ever watched someone talking about their holiday and, even though you have a killer anecdote to add to the conversation, you don't, in case no one wants to hear it? So often we have a window available to us to take part, to speak, to contribute, to be seen, and we deflect it; we pass the ball or quite literally hide behind our iPad, carefully reading each word we have prepared to be sure we make the 'right' contribution.

For the majority of us, even those of us who speak publicly or take the spotlight for a living, speaking at a gathering (whether that is 10 or 1,000 people) takes a bit of a push. It doesn't come naturally, the ability to address a large crowd. Those stand-up comics you see, joking with ease on TV, are not just naturally brilliant at entertaining the masses. They will have been working the comedy circuit for years, learning how to earn and keep an audience's attention and how not to collapse in terror when they walk out in front of a load of people. This doesn't mean that they don't feel scared, but that they can work through that feeling and not let it affect their performance. It follows, then, that if we aren't prepared or are less practised in having the room's gaze on us, even the thought of standing in front of a room of people can cause us to panic in the moment and imagine ourselves drowning in a sea of eyes. We need to practise holding spaces if we want to have an impact when we are taking up space for real.

Holding the Space

What do I mean by 'holding the space'? I mean literally taking responsibility for the energy* of the room. In the world of improv, we often speak of the energy that we, the performers, exchange. When you have a great chat with a friend which bounces to and fro, you are exchanging energy, alternating who is responsible for it. Think of a pal telling you excitedly about their new love, and how you absorb their excitement and send that energy back while you delightfully interrogate this new chapter in their life†. That energy is held by the person who has the focus of the conversation.

If you are delivering a monologue rather than in a conversation, you will need to keep that energy – that focus – for the room, until the monologue is over. A stand-up comic is holding the space when they do a comedy routine. If people stop listening or leave the theatre, she is no longer holding the space. If a heckler shouts and gets the better of her, she is no longer holding the space – the heckler is. If she does a killer line back at the heckler, she may win the crowd back and therefore be holding the space once more. We can hold the

---

* Some people balk at the use of the word 'energy'. You can use a different word if you wish. 'Fizz' or 'focus' are good substitutes.

† If you have been in a long relationship, like me, you will feed off these stories like a romance vampire. 'Tell me about when they held your hand for the first time again' you demand, whist eating popcorn like you are in a movie theatre.

space lightly, too – such as a counsellor would at an AA meeting. They invite others to contribute, but they are responsible for the flow of the discussion. You could say they are 'minding' the space; taking care of it while people work through what they wish to contribute to the group.

In improv workshops, if the participants don't realise that they are holding the space, we feel the energy dissipate. You will have felt this when you've been in a group conversation and an awkward topic has come up. Someone is talking about a painful experience or wants to discuss a strong opinion they hold. People often clam up because no one is quite sure what to say. No one is 'holding the space' for the conversation. The energy has dissipated. Once you've had these disappointing energy transfer experiences, it is no wonder you shy away from future ones.

Joining in

The first obstacle to joining in is often not being sure whose turn it is. There is a saying in improv land: 'If you're wondering whose turn it is, it's yours!' I first came across this brilliantly obvious idea in Jill Bernard's wonderful book, *Small Cute Book of Improv*, and it is one of my favourites. Our social indoctrination to be polite and kind humans often works against us being fully ourselves – stopping us responding to our instinct to take part and speak up. We use 'After you' as a way of protecting us from embarrassment and exposure. What is viewed as 'good manners' is, in fact, a stalling technique, used to avoid having to reveal all the uniqueness of you.

This stalling happens when playing improv games early on – when the game isn't comfortable yet, and part of the premise will involve putting something of yourself out there – a word, a sound or a movement. In the game 'sound ball' the participants have to offer a sound – whatever comes out of their mouth – and send it with an imaginary energy ball to another person in the group. People say they 'can't think of a sound' or hold the imaginary ball in their hands while they decide what sound will be best. It's a ridiculous game where no sound can be wrong and yet suddenly having the eyes of the group on them makes the player freeze and anxiously run through every sound they have ever made to find the 'right' one.

I see this happen in life all the time. I am part of a book club where no one ever wants to be the first to answer the question, 'How did you find the book?' in case everyone else thought differently. On video conference calls you see it when no one is officially hosting so everyone sits in their little box, wondering what to do*. There are twelve faces staring back at you, no one quite sure who should speak next. Well guess what? You can speak next! You can put your voice in the space, even if it is just to ask what the agenda is or to start the ball

------

* Whatever you do, don't take this time to put a comedy background on your screen. It will be funny for a moment, and then you will inevitably have to talk about making redundancies with a picture of a clown in a hammock behind you.

rolling. The earlier you put your voice in the room, the easier it will be to speak subsequently.

If meetings give you the heebie-jeebies, try to make sure you've said something early on.

Just a 'hello' or a comment about the weather – literally anything, so you can see that when you speak, people are not horrified. In improv, if you hate a particular game or exercise, you quickly learn the best thing you can do is just get in there and have a go. You may not be the funniest or the quickest, but you will have been part of the show. The same applies for anything that you show up to. It is enough to be a part of it – don't try and win it.

The speaking-in-meetings heebie-jeebies usually come from having had a bad experience of offering ideas up in a non-supportive environment – the times where we did step forward and someone crushed us just as we were offering a part of ourselves. It's horrible. But the only way to move on from that experience is to say your ideas out loud again. To be curious about that experience and note what was happening. Was your idea actually not that great, or were you with people who didn't notice that their behaviour was discouraging or who actively wanted to belittle you?

I'll give you two short examples. When I was starting out in the world of comedy, I was invited to share some written sketch ideas with a production company. They said: 'Bring along any ideas you have, no matter how raw or undeveloped they are.' I took this at face value and presented my ideas to two folks who then mocked everything I presented. Their behaviour was not cool, but I was also very green and misjudged the situation to be one where it was safe to present raw ideas. Actually, these people needed to see a finished product from me, because we hadn't built up any trust between us and all mutual trust certainly disappeared after that meeting. We never worked together after that.

Later that same year, I was filming an advert where the concept involved me doing a lot of improvising*. The director said to me 'Just keep spitballing ideas. We have loads of time so we can just keep going till we find what we are all happy with.' After the first 20 minutes, the director said 'This is all so great, Pippa. I really loved it when you pretended to see someone off camera. Can we explore that idea a bit more?' So we did. We worked like this for eight hours and it was the most fun I have ever had on set. Seventy per cent of what came out of my mouth was total rubbish, but the director knew that to get to the thirty per cent, I had to spit the rubbish out first. His encouragement meant that I felt comfortable to let myself and my ideas be seen, so that we could get to the golden nuggets.

So, after those hugely contrasting experiences, I now double-check whether each meeting is one where I can genuinely show my unpolished work or if I am with people who need clear, thought-through ideas. That was my learning – but it was painful.

---

* I was the face of Microsoft Search, now Bing!, for several years. I know, I have had many strange and wonderful jobs. I recorded about 50 different films/books for an interactive game of charades. Great gig. Still excellent at charades.

Know what kind of meeting you are in. Know what is required of you, and then take up space in a way that will serve you.

Taking up Space in a Group

In workshop settings, it is particularly interesting when the energy drop occurs. We are playing a simple game and yet people don't step in to make the next move or join in, even though there is officially nothing to lose. We have agreed to fail at the beginning of the session, just as you did when you read that oath out loud*. We agreed that we could get all the exercises wrong, and yet we still don't step forward because we made that agreement to fail before we remembered what having a go feels like. Before we have a go, we get the same feeling as just before we fail – it is the feeling of not knowing exactly what will happen in the next moment. The feeling of embracing the unknown. And when we feel that flutter in our tummy, we often back away rather than step up, because fight or flight says: 'The group is going to turn on you if you get this wrong.' But if you don't step in to make the next move, the whole game falls apart. So there is a part of us that would rather the whole thing fail, that we collectively lose all momentum, rather than stick out our head and keep the conversation going with a slightly wonky offer.

---

* You did do the oath didn't you? If not, go back to page 27. Do not pass Go. Do not collect £200.

When these moments happen in workshops – the energy dropping and the game coming to a halt – I always ask, 'Who had an instinct to do something?' and about half the room will put up their hands. We'll talk through what they might have done if they had listened to themselves and 99 per cent of the suggestions would have been absolutely fine. They might not be golden nuggets for the group, revered for the rest of time, but they would have kept the game in play and offered something that might lead to a spectacular moment.

Collaboration, to the uninitiated, can be terrifying. We don't want to look stupid, we don't want to say anything too obvious, we perhaps put pressure on ourselves to say the thing that seals the deal. The best way to stop the runaway self-judgement train is to think about what you are aiming for collectively, rather than fixating on your personal contribution. Jill Bernard says, 'If you don't want to be in your head, be somewhere else instead', which I offer to you as a way to shift your focus from yourself to your team. Take the pressure off being brilliant and instead focus on making something brilliant happen, collectively.

What is this pressure for us to be amazing at all times? To come up with, in one immediate, succinct thought, the brilliant solution which will make us the saviour of the moment? We are living in a time that celebrates the individual. Where despite having whole teams behind them, the individual is lifted up as the winner, masking the collective that makes their apparent individual success occur. This isn't always done on purpose. We have been trained to celebrate the initiator rather than the team process. We prefer the simple narrative of James Dyson, the brilliant inventor who dreamed up and immediately executed his sexy vacuum* rather than the story of the teams of engineers, the fifteen years and the 5,000 prototypes of the Dyson, arguably the most famous vacuum cleaner of all time.

In *Showstopper! The Improvised Musical* we try to combat this individual need to be seen as brilliant by saying: 'Serve the show, not yourself'. We ask, 'What does the scene need?' rather than, 'What shall I do now?' By putting the focus on what we are creating collectively rather than looking for individual satisfaction, taking up space becomes less daunting, because you accept that the project is not solely on your shoulders. You are sharing the space, and as we contribute with the group aim in mind, the space expands to hold us all, rather than following individual players. I am not improvising a musical on my own, I am creating a musical with my nine most fabulous colleagues. We must hold the space together.

On a personal level, it might mean putting your idea into the world whilst recognising that your creation is not finished. It can be hard, because looking at our own half-formed ideas means accepting our inability to immediately articulate what it is we want to say or do. By working with these messy, ugly ideas, though, we can refine and create something brilliant.

---

* 'Sexy' is the correct adjective here. I don't know anyone who can look at a Dyson and not say, 'Oooh isn't it beautiful?' But then again, maybe I need to widen my circle of friends.

We do not have to be perfect to take up space, we only need to be present. You may not be the holder of a finished idea, but you will be on the map to finding it. So step up and let your voice be heard. You are part of the journey that leads to the treasure.

The way to get things done is not to mind who gets the credit of doing them – Old Proverb*

Stepping up

Physically stepping into a space can be a big deal for a lot of people. That moment when you have to step forward and give a presentation, or the celebrant says, 'Do you take this man to be your husband?' or someone at a dinner party says, 'Pippa, you're funny. Tell us a joke!†' Notice that burn in your belly and remember that fear and excitement create a similar energy. Think of that feeling as rocket fuel and step forward, my friend. Your body is providing you with the petrol to take the space. Deliver the speech knowing that you deserve to be there.

Say 'I do!' unless you don't. Tell the joke and punch your friend later.

---

* Ironically, this proverb is credited to several people, including Harry S. Truman (president of the United States) and Benjamin Jowett (Oxford lecturer). Hope they aren't fighting in the afterlife.

† Never do this to your friend who is a comedian. They will not thank you. Or be able to think of something funny.

If taking up space is something that you find incredibly difficult, be kind to yourself and take it in tiny steps. Everyone works at a different pace. Some people get over a fear of heights by jumping out of a plane and others do it by stepping up a ladder, one rung at a time.

We all have something to offer, big or small. In an improv show you might be a tree making a scene look beautiful or you might be a main character. Either way, you were part of the show and the final piece was not possible without the individual offers.

So, take up space. Hold the space. Know you deserve to be seen and heard.

Open up the Space for Others

At university, I was talking to my friend, Tom. We were chatting about something that had happened the night before and I said, 'Well that's because you're so shy.'

And he said, 'I'm not shy, I just don't feel the need to talk all the frickin' time.'

Isn't it nice when friends don't mince their words? He lives in Australia now where he has lots of space to be as quiet as he likes and doesn't have to wait for me to finish my third monologue of the day to get a word in. Hi Tom!

For those of us who love to speak, who are comfortable in meetings, who waltz around parties gracefully and love love love to be in the presence of others, it is important that we notice if perhaps we have taken all the space and aren't offering it to others.

Go and see any improv night and I promise there will be someone who is in EVERY SINGLE SCENE and once you notice it, it isn't half annoying. There's a scene about an ice cream van and oh! Look who's come to order a cone, it's That Guy! And now there's a new scene about two chickens fighting over some grain and who's come to sort out the argument? It's That Guy! That Guy isn't just in improv scenes. He is in your office, offering unsolicited advice and getting involved with every committee that exists. Occasionally, this will be because that person is unable to imagine that their help isn't needed, but mostly, they will have no idea they are doing it*. They might be being 'helpful' because they are working with less experienced people or they might be so drunk on audience appreciation that they can't stop themselves going in for another laugh. When you are able to take space and hold space, it can be hard to open up the space for others.

This took me a long time to learn. I was lucky that my first improv group proper† was made up of people who were all

---

* Another great side learn from improv is knowing that most people have no idea what additional behaviours they are engaging in when they are performing. Improv taught me that people aren't out to get you, they are mostly unaware. So next time someone is picking their nose next to you, just say, 'Do you mind not doing that?' because, most likely, they have no idea that they just rammed their finger deep up their nostril.

† Scratch Improv – an Edinburgh hit for five years with The Reduced Edinburgh Fringe Improv Show where we would get the audience to rip shows out of the Edinburgh brochure and then improvise them for the audience, so they could see all the shows they wanted to see at the Fringe, in an hour. Loved it.

more experienced than me. As a newbie, I got to learn on the job with people who were already pretty good. These generous people opened a door for me because they could see some raw talent. After my initial 'new girl' status had begun to wear off, I started fearing anyone coming into my improv spaces because they might be better than me. If someone was guesting with us in a show or I was asked to be a guest in a show, I would find myself secretly enjoying if someone was not as funny or quick as me, because it meant I didn't feel threatened. It didn't feel good, but I couldn't stop myself.

With hindsight, I can see it was because I hadn't yet accepted that my contributions were truly welcome and that I was trusted. Until we find our own true self-belief and allow ourselves to embody it, it is hard to open our spaces to others, because we fear we might be replaced, that by sharing the spotlight we will, somehow, be forgotten. This idea that there is not enough space for everyone is entirely driven by fear. In my case, fear that I might not be as enjoyable to the audience if there was someone else in the group who was as funny as me. Instead of believing in myself, I was feeding off other people believing in me. I was trying to keep other people down or out of the way so I wouldn't have to share the audience praise that was my only fuel.

But when we try to keep other people down, all that happens is people go off and find other spaces to grow in. Those people get better at their craft, and then because they haven't had a good experience being in the same space as us, they don't feel keen to invite us to their party. Those people I wasn't welcoming to didn't invite me to play in their new, exciting spaces. So who missed out in the end? Little old Pippa Evans. If you don't let anyone else in the sandpit, then you have no one to turn into a sand mermaid. And it isn't so fun making a tail and seashell bra by yourself.

When we are in charge of a space – whether that is hosting a creative meeting at work, having friends round for dinner or teaching an aerobics class* – how are we making sure that everyone we've invited feels welcome in the space?

The first offer I have for you is: acknowledge people. This might be through eye contact, naming everyone or asking for a verbal contribution up top. If it is a group that you regularly meet with, you might be aware of the different ways people like to contribute. So, Rhea loves to talk – you can give her a minute and make it clear when it's time for her to stop. James is shy so just an eye contact acknowledgement might be more comfortable for him. Meg might respond best to a stimulus like being asked a question, so oblige them that. Notice the people in your space and let them know that they are welcome.

This may seem obvious, but it is so often overlooked. Improvisers would never go on stage to improvise a show together without at the very least having looked each other in the eye. We are about to share some space together and create something by offering a part of ourselves. Our ideas, our thoughts, our gifts. Giving something of yourself is a

---

* Seriously, I have no idea who is reading this, so I am covering all bases.

vulnerable thing to do and we are less likely to participate in this way if we don't feel welcome in the space. It is no different when you are gathering to discuss a new political bill or design the latest electric car*.

To take up space, we must believe in ourselves and the value we add to any activity simply by showing up. Once we feel able to take up space, it is imperative that we simultaneously feel able to share that space. Only once we can show up fully, and value others and their contributions, will we feel we are contributing to our own story and the story of the group.

---

* I may not know who is reading the book, but I do have lofty ideas about them.

Exercise Corner

SOLO

Small steps to practise taking up space:

1. Stand or sit in a park, in the middle of an open piece of land and look forward to the horizon or a lovely tree. Feet planted, hands on hips, breathe in the air and know you can stay here as long as you want. If you feel self-conscious, acknowledge that feeling but stay where you are for just a bit longer than you want to. Congratulations. You have taken up space.

2. Go to a supermarket and ask someone to pass you an item off the shelf. Congratulations! You have been seen. You have taken up space in the world.

3. Give a compliment to someone at a bus stop. Congratulations! You have seen them, and they will see you. You might even get a compliment back. Nice.

4. If you work in an office environment, speak to people rather than email them. This might mean going over to their desk in a physical office or calling them on the phone. This will not only improve your relationships, but help you know you are worthy of people's time, which is taking up space.

IN A GROUP

Make a circle. One person will step into the middle of the space and tell the group something about themselves. It could be as simple as what they had for breakfast or something more personal like a challenge they are facing. When the person is finished, they return to their spot and when they have arrived back, the circle gives them a round of applause.

It is VITAL that the applause isn't given until they have returned to their spot, because it is the walk into the centre of the space and back to our starting position that is the most naked moment for the participant. In this tiny walk, we are not speaking, we are simply being observed. Here we show the group that we are taking the space and then that we are relinquishing the space back to the group. Observe how you walk into the space. So many people hop into the middle or start talking as soon as they leave their starting position because they cannot bear the silence and the attention on them.

When speaking, it can be hard – if you are not used to speaking free-form – to know how to end. I suggest that you simply say 'the end' when you are done. Knowing you are finished will give permission for you to make a clear exit, instead of sliding back to your spot on an 'Um' or a 'So that's me then . . .' A clear ending instead of petering out.

Though it sounds simple, this exercise is one that people frequently tell me they find the most challenging, because it asks you to take up space, speak about yourself, and decide when you are ready to finish. No one tells you when to go into the space, you must follow your intuition that it is 'your turn'.

Once the person who has gone first has returned and their applause has been given, anyone else can take the space. Here is where the second lull happens (the first being when the offer is made that anyone can go into the space to start the exercise) as no one immediately steps in; it is not clear whose turn it is. Remember the mantra: if you don't know whose turn it is, it's yours!

Another thing that can occur is two people trying to go into the space at the same time and then having to negotiate who is going. We are embarrassed that we had the same impulse. We were not original. We ruined the other person's idea. You did not! It is a beautiful thing for two people to have the same impulse – like when you bump into someone in the street and both try to let the other pass by. We do a little dance and then we are on our way. How often we laugh in that little dance, finding joy in our mutual attempt to let the other go, our both having the same impulses to go left or right. Our wish to be original stops our joy at having a spark with a fellow human. Take a moment to acknowledge the similar impulse. Then offer the space or take the space. It is as simple as that.

What Is This REALLY About?

When we first started doing *Showstopper! The Improvised Musical*, we would often have scenes which were rambling and all over the place. We would be two police officers making cups of tea, talking about the weather, chatting in a way that wasn't about much and wasn't really going anywhere. It would happen all the time, in front of audiences who we could feel were starting to get restless as they weren't being entertained or intrigued or thrilled.

So we devised the plan that if we sensed this was happening, one of the characters would say to another, 'What is this really about?', at which point the other character would have to say something more than, 'Would you like sugar?'

Instead it might be, 'I need to tell you I am leaving', 'I'm having an affair', 'I did kill that guy – the gun was mine' or, 'I love you!'

We would have to commit to something and get to the meat of the scene. And it worked.

I think about this often when I am procrastinating. When I am making my seventeenth cup of tea instead of writing or when I know I need to make a difficult phone call but instead I have decided now is the time to defrost the freezer. And so, when I notice that I am suddenly moved to take up learning a foreign language instead of doing what I need to do, I say to myself loud and clear:

Pippa! What is this really about?

And usually the answer is, 'I am scared of what might happen if I make the call' or, 'I don't think I can write a book.' And once I have said the true, deeper thought out loud, it sounds a lot less frightening. So if you find yourself going for a sixth biscuit when you know that isn't what you really need, I encourage you to put down the biscuit tin and say:

What is this really about?

Out loud.

To yourself.

And you will know.

And then you can move on.

Once you know what is causing you to avoid the thing, you can accept the block for what it is: a thought, a feeling.

And then you can face it.

What is this really about?

It's about naming your fears, so they have less of a grip on you, and confronting them.

LET'S TALK ABOUT YES

Pretty much everyone who walks through the door at an Improv Your Life class wants to talk about the word YES. Whether it is never saying it or saying it too much or saying it but not meaning it, never has our relationship been more complicated with a word than it is with this one.

YES has an interesting place in Western culture, and particularly within a world which idolises achieving everything by the time you are 25 and retiring with a yacht to write your memoirs because there is nothing more to achieve; you've done it all already. Congratulations, hardly anyone*!

In our hurry to succeed, YES is often jumped upon as the way to get to the end. Say YES to all opportunities that come your way, without question and surely you will win the game of life. However, for most of us, we don't beat the boss and win the game. There is no yacht†. Or we get the yacht and yet don't feel that

---

* Helpful tip if you feel like you haven't managed to be Richard Branson. Count the number of people like Richard Branson. Not that many. Sure, it would be nice to own an island, but I struggle to hoover my front room. Wouldn't want to hoover a whole island as well.

† Insert own personal yacht-type item if yacht is not working for you. Personal massage assistant or self-tying shoes like in Back to the Future Part II.

tasty satisfaction the movies said we would. There is just another load of things to say YES to and we burn out, or fizzle out, or both.

Most experiences of burnout can be put down to the word YES. In our wish to be generous, kind, giving humans, or forward-thinking, successful idea-embracers, we find ourselves saying YES to more than we can deal with, and then often resent what it is we are now committed to. Our tick lists are huge, because the thought of saying NO is too complicated. It will involve disappointing people. It will mean we have to have difficult conversations. We are too tired to say NO, but if we said NO we might have a chance at being less tired.

In his seminal book, *Impro*, Keith Johnstone says, 'There are people who say yes and people who say no. One leads to adventure, the other safety.' This is a great quote because it doesn't say YES is better than NO or vice versa, just that they lead in different directions. However, if we always follow left and never right, we move in circles. So let's look at our relationship with YES, to check that we aren't creating tornadoes for ourselves.

YES

I am terrible for saying YES to too much. It is still something I have to work on, constantly. Because I love doing things and being involved. I am really good at getting things done and making things work. But I have, too many times, collapsed with exhaustion and wondered why that was, only to remember that I was being so generous with my time that I forgot to keep some for myself.

In one of my favourite books, *The Artist's Way*, Julia Cameron talks about 'overfishing the pond' of your personal resources. So when I find myself, yet again, needing to go to sleep but trying to finish that song I promised I would write my Dad's friend's brother for their boss's birthday, I say to myself, 'Are you overfishing the pond, Pips?' And I have to say, 'Yes'.

So it is no wonder that people arrive at Improv Your Life wondering about YES. I know when I started improvising all those years ago, I had never thought about it as having a pivotal role in my daily life. But improv really lets you explore the relationship with YES in a place where the consequences are imaginary – and that is such a gift. You have to say YES to other people's ideas, and they have to say YES to yours. Where else do you get to try out life in an imaginary world but with real people? However, if you are struggling with the amount you already say YES to, the thought of a whole practice based around the word can be daunting.

When we say YES, we open ourselves up to ideas, adventure and creativity. We also open ourselves up to be vulnerable, malleable and influenced by what is happening around us. In a way, we give up a little bit of control. We put a foot out in front of us without knowing what will happen next, and that is thrilling.

YES AND

If you have ever gone to a beginner's improv class, you will 99 per cent of the time, learn YES AND. YES AND is a traditional improv exercise to build on another's ideas and to experience total acceptance. We have to work in agreement to get anywhere together – so we start building with YES.

The exercise looks like this: two improvisers work together in a pair, and one starts with a statement.

Person A: Let's go to the beach!

From here on, all sentences start with YES AND:

Person B: Yes! And we can take a picnic!
Person A: Yes! And we can lay it out on a blanket!
Person B: Yes! And we can invite all the neighbours.
Person A: Yes! And we can invite the seagulls.
Person B: Yes! And we'll all eat the picnic together!

You can create a whole world so quickly with YES AND:

Person A: Let's start a new country!
Person B: Yes! And it will be free for everyone to live in!
Person A: Yes! And we'll give cupcakes to everyone as they arrive!
Person B: Yes! And the bakers will sing as they craft their wares!
Person A: Yes! And everyone in our new country will be able to sing!
Person B: Yes! And we'll call it Singing Country!

See how quickly we got a whole scenario? Six lines and we have a new country. Such a great exercise for visualising ideas, writing stories and letting our imaginations go as far as they can possibly go. If we never YES AND our thoughts, we stifle them and can start to believe we have no imagination. That we are not creative. YES AND frees us from that fear. We realise there is potential where previously we were told there was none.

YES AND is a fantastic exercise because it helps us notice when we stall:

Person A: Let's go to the beach!
Person B: Yes. And maybe we . . . can . . . make . . . a . . . castle?

See how **Person B** has turned their idea into a question? Why are they asking permission? It's a made-up situation. And yet, despite having permission to do anything, we stall because suddenly we are responsible for a part of the plan. Suddenly, someone is going to hear a part of how your brain works. And that can be terrifying. But we are in the world of YES AND. Your partner *has* to agree with you! So spit out whatever you want to say, because they are going to go with it, no matter how terrible you think it is.

It reveals our resistance to other people's ideas:

Person A: Yes! And we can BBQ fish!
Person B: Yes! And we can not do that, too!

Just because you don't like BBQs in real life, doesn't mean they can't exist in the imaginary world of this beach trip. YES AND reveals a fear of being judged on someone else's idea. You can see this on stage in an improv show, when someone raises their eyebrow at an offer another player makes. They are endowed as a pirate and they sneer and say, 'Yes, I'm a pirate. Because we are, what, five years old?' instead of just

YES AND-ing them and having a swashbuckling time. Standing outside the idea is so much easier than getting onboard, because then we can't be held accountable.

When we panic that we have nothing to say:

Person A: Let's go to the beach!

Person B: Yes! And . . . oh, I don't know. I can't think of anything.

If you have ever been told you are not creative, that you weren't good at art, that you are very practical but have no imagination – being suddenly asked for an idea can be overwhelming. It is similar to the questioning response in that it is a belief that your idea won't be very good. It is a protection to say, 'I have no idea,' because then, again, you can't be seen. But by not revealing anything of yourself, other than you won't join in fully, you are cutting yourself off from living fully. You are telling yourself that your ideas have no value. And, by extension, that neither do you.

By observing these things, we can start to notice if they are just down to nerves when learning a new skill, or habits that we take into life. When someone asks for your input, do you stall? Do you question your own ideas? Do you sneer at the original idea? If your colleague suggests a new way of organising the filing system, do you always revert to: 'That will never work'? If your partner asks you what colour you'd like to paint the lounge, do you always ask them what colour they want first?

This exercise is revealing in so many ways, because so often we find ways around putting ourselves out there. We stop ideas before they have even begun, because we don't say YES AND. We say YES BUT.

YES BUT

YES BUT is the friend of the polite person who wants to be seen to be agreeing but isn't. YES BUT translates as: 'I like your idea but also I don't'. Recognise that guy? Sneaky little so-and-so, isn't he?

Let's see the same exercise again with YES BUT.

Person A: Let's go to the beach!

Person B: Yes, but I don't like beaches.

Person A: Yes, but this one is special.

Person B: Yes, but special things intimidate me.

Person A: Yes, but you need to get over that.

Person B: Yes, but you don't own me.

Person A: Yes, but I am responsible for you right now.

And on and on and on . . .

YES BUT is tiring and it doesn't go anywhere. We are at loggerheads. As one tries to sell their idea, the other defends their position. If we are trying to create something – whether we are designing a new app for the iPhone or trying to decide where to go on holiday, YES BUT can stop the ideas from even starting.

Person A: Let's go on holiday!

Person B: Yes, but we can't afford it.

Person A: Yes, but we can try and find the money.

Person B: Yes, but we need to be responsible.

Person A: Yes, but if we don't see if it's possible, we'll never know.

Person B: Yes, but anything is possible, including bankruptcy.

We haven't got past whether we can even consider the idea, let alone started to explore the idea itself.

When I teach YES AND and YES BUT, I ask the class to notice how it feels to be told YES AND or say YES AND. Then to compare how it feels to say or hear YES BUT. YES AND feels energising, exciting, thrilling even, while YES BUT feels frustrating, halting and like a slap in the face. Once you recognise the feel of these phrases, you can notice the essence of them in your day to day. Because, most likely, in real life you can be behaving in a YES AND or YES BUT manner, without using the actual phrases.

For example:

Person A: (running in, excited) I got a bonus from work!

Person B: Well that's going to get taxed. (YES BUT)

Person A: Only a bit. Means we can get the new garden furniture. (YES AND-ing themselves)

Person B: If it's still for sale. It was very popular. (YES BUT)

Person A: Maybe I'll just give the bonus back. (YES AND-ing Person B)

Person B: Why are you being such a downer? (What a doughnut)

See how Person B is bringing this conversation down when Person A came in with such energy? This is YES BUT in action. Person B is pointing out all the reasons why Person A shouldn't be excited. Person A will probably think twice about telling Person B any good news ever again.

By noticing how it feels to say and hear YES AND and YES BUT, you are more likely to notice when you are falling into those patterns, or someone you are speaking with is. And then you can choose how you want to play it. Are you here to create or to stall? Notice what is happening, then choose how you want to move forward.

Is YES BUT Always Bad?

Nothing is absolute (apart from the vodka). However, YES BUT is a habit that often needs to be broken before it can be in any way useful. YES BUT is so often our defender that we can be saying it without noticing. That's why it often appears when first playing the YES AND exercise. It is such a reflex that we find ourselves saying it even when we have been given explicit instructions to just say YES AND.

It's like anything we do without realising – first, you have to notice it. I remember doing a mock interview for university and the person interviewing me started just repeating: 'LIKE LIKE LIKE LIKE' and I didn't know what was going on. She pointed out that every third word I was saying was 'like'. After that, I became really aware of it and, like, it was, like really bonkers, like, the amount I, like, said, 'like'. So now I don't say 'like' every other word, but I haven't banned it from my vocabulary, like.

YES BUT can be useful as a phrase in negotiation. This is particularly true if you are the practical part of a team. The creatives on a project want to do X and Y but you know that will take six years your company doesn't have. The kids want to go to Disneyland® but you don't have the money. These are reasonable YES BUTs to bring in. However, we often bring YES BUT in too early, stifling the project before the idea has had time to come to life.

> **Creatives:** We've got this idea for a bridge over the
> English Channel.
> **Project Manager:** YES BUT there's no time.
> **Creatives:** We worked on this for ages, and you won't
> even hear us out?
> **Project Manager:** (fingers in ears) I am sorry, I am having
> trouble hearing you.
>
> **Kids:** Let's go to Disneyland®.
> **Parent:** YES BUT we can't afford it.
> **Kids:** You are the worst!

However, if we allow the idea to develop a little and we work with YES AND (agreement and expansion), we can bring out what the essence of the idea is and then, if we need to adapt it for practical reasons, we have more details to work with. So often, the reason YES BUT irks the receiver is because it has come seemingly out of nowhere. An instant NO in disguise. But it's not as clear as a NO, so there is a disconnect with the receiver. A feeling of being fobbed off rather than spoken to honestly. If we allow the idea to live for a little longer, YES BUT can be a reshaping tool, rather than a deflater. A way to open up a side door rather than an emergency exit.

Kids: Let's go to Disneyland®.

Parent: (YES AND attitude) Disneyland® looks like a really fun place.

Kids: Yes. We want to see Mickey and ride on Space Mountain.

Parent: (YES AND attitude) Space Mountain is a roller coaster, right? I love roller coasters.

Kids: Yes – we want to go really fast.

Parent: (YES BUT) Unfortunately, we don't have the money to go all the way to America.

Kids: But it's not fair!

Parent: (YES BUT) But you know where else they have roller coasters? Alton Towers.

Kids: Mickey Mouse isn't there.

Parent: (YES BUT) No, but we would be!

Kids: Great idea, Dad. Group hug*!

YES BUT is not an evil phrase, it is simply overused and often, badly timed. So be sure to notice when it is popping out and if it is what you want to say, or if it is acting on your behalf without you asking it to.

---

* I don't have children, but I imagine this is a pretty accurate portrayal of negotiating with kids.

YES Goes Solo

Cheerleaders are fantastic. They stand at the sidelines and encourage you. They are YES-ing your every move. They make the team feel great and they do it while standing on each other's shoulders and doing backflips. Hooray for cheerleaders! This is a pure YES and so welcome when we are just needing encouragement.

But this YES can become the most frustrating when a cheerleader isn't the only function required of us. 'I am with you,' we say, 'but I won't add my own ideas. I don't want to hold the responsibility for this.' A way to show willing without opening ourselves up to rejection.

> **Person A:** Let's go to the beach!
> **Person B:** Yes!
> **Person A:** Cool. I'll get the car.
> **Person B:** Yes!
> **Person A:** Shall I buy the gas?
> **Person B:** Yes!
> **Person A:** Am I doing all the donkey work?
> **Person B:** Yes!

This is so one-sided and often hard to challenge, because Person B is being really nice. They are also not contributing, and if you are creating something you are supposed to be working on together, this YES can get very tiring.

I remember a time when I was a kid, and I was supposed to work on a school project with another girl, Anna

Thomas*, about rainforests. But I wasn't very interested, and I just kinda didn't do anything. So Anna would ask me if I'd do something and I'd say YES, but then not really follow it up.

In the end, Anna created most of the project. She wrote her name at the top of everything she had written or drawn, to show that I had done nothing when it came to being marked. Harsh. But I get it. I was a weight she was carrying and no matter how nice and positive I was, I wasn't doing what I had said I would: some of the work.

If you find yourself saying YES a lot – being encouraging but not putting much of yourself into the picture – check-in and see if something else might be needed from you. If you aren't putting that AND on the end, just be curious as to why. There might be something else lurking behind its absence.

YES Isn't a Word, It's an Attitude

We have covered these three types of YES:

YES – Encouraging/agreeing
YES AND – Adding and building
YES BUT – Questioning and stalling

---

* Funny how you remember your childhood friends' full names, isn't it? Especially when most people's names in my phone now are like 'Sikisa Comedy' or 'Daniel Pub IGNORE AT ALL COSTS'

In every class, there is always one student who will question me once we have covered these three types of YES. 'Pippa,' they say, 'I am going to look insane if I start every sentence with YES AND! It's just not practical!' and a few others murmur in agreement. This is when I like to make it clear that these exercises are just that – exercises. They are honing in on something fundamental and exaggerating it so that we can investigate it. Like a microscope in a lab. And now we are going to zoom out and I am going to ask you to move on from thinking of these YES's as words to be used in a meeting, a discussion or an argument, and now expand the phrase YES AND as a mindset to approach living your life.

When we start learning improv, we have to start by building trust. Allowing people to be creative in ways that expand potential, rather than create perfection. This is why most improv courses start with YES AND. And so do most friendships and relationships (you love everything each other says, you go along to events without question, you eat their food without mentioning you are allergic to kiwi fruit and just pretend you have injected lip fillers in the bathroom). It is when the trust of YES AND is broken – when it is questioned too early – that our relationships can start to falter.

The concept of YES AND is not here to help you live a delusional life, but rather one that is open to possibility. One that allows us to imagine scenarios that have not presented themselves yet. Instead of saying, 'Oh I could never do that,' when your friend says you should ask out Barry at work, or apply for that new position that would mean moving to Sydney, YES AND allows you to entertain that possibility. To expand it in your imagination and feel, for a second, what it might be like. A YES AND mindset enables us not to fear the unknown, but to be curious about it instead.

If it wasn't for YES AND, I wouldn't have travelled the world teaching and performing improvisation. If it wasn't for YES AND, I wouldn't be writing this book. I wouldn't have stopped hating on myself and living in constant fear that someone was going to think I was an idiot.

Brain: People will think you're an idiot, Pippa!
Pippa: YES, AND they might be right. But at least this way, we get to find out for sure.

The only time YES is your foe is when we are saying YES when we don't mean it.

Which is why the next chapter is dedicated to saying NO.

Exercise Corner

This week, notice whenever you say YES, YES AND or YES BUT. Don't change it, just notice it. Write it down in a notebook (or on your phone) and at the end of the day, go through them all. Think about what made you say which YES. Were you happy to say YES in that moment? How was your YES met? Perhaps you always say YES to work but rarely to social engagements. Perhaps you say YES rarely and want to think about why that is.

Once you have a feel for your YES pattern, change it up.

See what it feels like to say YES more.

See if you can slip a few YES ANDs into conversations.

Try out some YES BUTs and notice the effect they have on the people around you.

Play with YES as a word and an attitude.

You might just surprise yourself with where you end up.

OUR OLD FRIEND NO

Oh no. Oh no, oh no, oh no, oh no.

My mum always likes to talk about when I was a kid and I learnt the word 'no'. Or as I said, 'note'. If my dad asked me to do something, I would look at him and smile with my big blue eyes and blond curls and I would reply, 'Note'. And he could do nothing. Because I had refused. And I was so cute.

When we are small, NO is the first word we utter where we feel real power. Parents dread their child learning it, because then they have to learn to negotiate. When a kid says NO, what can you do? Do you want to go and play outside? NO. Tidy your room. NO. It is a shield in the battle of doing what we want to do, all of the time. Cartoons and crisps at dawn, forever!

But as grown-ups, we can find that NO has rather become a habit. Several people come on my course wishing to figure out why they say NO all the time. They have become masters at creating strong boundaries that keep them safe. So good at saying NO, people have perhaps stopped asking them to come to events. So good at saying NO, they don't cope very well with change to their routine, because it so rarely happens. By getting so good at saying NO, they have limited their experiences and see that it might actually be restricting them somehow.

And whilst those folks are wanting to stop saying NO, there are those of us who have a painful relationship with NO. Because there were so many times we wanted to say NO but we didn't. Or we said it and someone didn't hear it. NO wasn't our friend, because it was supposed to look after us and it didn't. Or perhaps, more painfully, we tried to look after ourselves and we couldn't.

When was the last time you said 'NO'? NO to family, NO to friends, NO to work or NO to yourself. How did it feel? Did it go hitch free? Saying NO to the coffee shop server when they ask if you want sugar can be easy, but saying NO when your friends want to go to an expensive restaurant and you can't afford it can be hard – when the NO comes with consequences.

Those of us who were brought up to be kind and generous often struggle to say NO because it feels like a selfish word. We look at our diaries and say:

'Sure, I can help you with that document, Kailash. Working late is my jam!'

'I am pretty busy, Jo, but I could meet you on Friday between three and four if I don't have any lunch.'

We fear what the NO says about us, so we rarely say it. It might be seen as saying we are more important than Kailash's work. We might never get asked for coffee by Jo again. People might think we consider our time to be precious, but not their friendship.

Here's the thing: NO is a form of SELF-LOVE*.

Hold onto this idea for a moment, because we need to see NO as self-serving in a positive way. Because actually NO is a YES to <u>yourself</u>.

It is true. We fail to say NO most of the time because we fear the consequences.

'I can't come to dinner,' might mean never being invited again.

'I don't have time to play with you,' might lead your children to resent you.

'I don't want what you want,' might cause your partner to question your compatibility.

But in all these situations, saying NO is saying YES to your truth, and therefore the truth of the situation. When is NO a YES? When it will serve everyone better in the situation.

Example:

Partner you are not that into: Marry me!
You: It's a NO from me.

This NO is a YES! Because you shouldn't marry someone you don't want to. Yes, they will be hurt, yes they will be angry, but ultimately, NO is the right choice.

This is a big, life-moment example, but it is also true for so many tiny things.

---

* Danger. She's started using hippie phrases again. Is this a cult†?
† Too late to be asking this now, my friend. Take a drink from the chalice . . .

You are asked to complete a task at work you don't have time for today.

Say NO. You will do a much better job if you do it tomorrow.

Your friend has invited you to a party, but you are exhausted.

Say NO. You will see your friend another time and have a proper catch up.

You have given up booze for January but your mates are all trying to get you to break it.

Say NO. Ultimately, they will be impressed by your will-power. They are just worried that if you can do it, so could they.

So often in improv class, when we are doing scenes, students will agree to do something in the scene because they have misunderstood the concept of YES AND, thinking they have to say YES to every detail, when the word NO might actually make for a more nuanced, rich scene.

Example: Two New York gangsters stand outside a children's home.

(Please imagine this dialogue in thick New York accents.)

Gangster 1: Let's blow up this orphanage!
Gangster 2: (awkwardly) Great idea!

I will interrupt and say to Person 1, 'Do you want to blow up the orphanage? Because your face didn't seem to suggest you did.' And the student will say they didn't, but they thought they had to YES AND Person 1's idea. Then I'll explain that you can say NO to the offer whilst YES AND-ing the situation.

Person 1 can still blow up the orphanage. You don't have to stop the scene to say what you want to say.

> **Gangster 1:** Let's blow up the orphanage!
>
> **Gangster 2:** Hmm, I don't know. Now we've got the dynamite, I am not into the idea. My favourite musical's *Annie*. I'd hate to think we're blowing up all the potential Annie's of the world.
>
> **Gangster 1:** Give me that dynamite. I can't get a break around here!
>
> **Gangster 2:** Geez, Mikey. Can't believe you're gonna blow up the place that was your home for ten years.
>
> **Gangster 1:** Yeah. Ten years I'll never get back.

Well, this is a far more interesting scene than two people just blowing up an orphanage, because both characters are speaking their truth. Person 2 is having doubts, and so shows them. Person 1 can still follow their original idea. They can YES AND their individual character's idea and YES AND the actor's offer, even though it sounds like a NO.

This is about YES AND-ing your truth, which will sometimes involve saying NO. If your truth is that you are tired and need to rest, saying NO to an invitation to go out dancing is hearing your tiredness and saying YES to rest. If your truth is you can't go on an overnight business trip because you haven't spent much time with your kids lately, saying NO is a YES to wanting to be a good parent. This is NO as a YES.

When we say NO to something we don't want to do, we are saying YES to the offer we are making to ourselves.

NO as a Block

NO is a block if it denies the reality of the situation.

NO is a block if it does not offer an alternative or a way to continue the discussion.

> **Person 1:** Let's go out for dinner.
>
> **Person 2:** No – I hate eating out.
>
> **Person 1:** We ate out yesterday.
>
> **Person 2:** No we didn't!
>
> **Person 1:** We did – you had a pizza. You said it was delicious.
>
> **Person 2:** Well, I hated it. And I hate you! *Runs into the distance.*

Have you ever done something like this? Exaggerated your feelings about something to make your point, rather than just being open to the complexity of your feelings?

When our NO comes out of nowhere and offers nowhere to go, that is when it leads to communication breakdown. It is not the word that is the issue, but rather how we are delivering the word. Think about the last time you were told NO in a way that didn't feel good. Why was it annoying or upsetting? I imagine it was because it wasn't clear why it was said or where it came from.

In my classes, I like to get my students to improvise with themselves. This is because you suddenly experience first-hand a) what you are actually saying and b) what it is like to work with you.

On one occasion, I had a student who would constantly say NO to other classmates' offers. When I pointed this out to her, she did not agree. 'I am simply making the narrative more interesting.' Which is fair, if the scene carries on, but often they stopped dead because the NO was strong, brutal, came out of nowhere and left the other improviser flailing around. So I got her to improvise with herself, playing two characters of her choice. We set the scene in a dress shop.

Character 1: Hello – are you open?
Character 2: No. We are closed. Come back later.

This was a great moment – because suddenly my student was faced with her own NO. The class sat in anticipation – what will happen next? Character 1 came back with:

Character 1: Are you sure?
Character 2: Yes. I'll be open at 10.

I challenged my student. 'Why not have the shop open? This is a scene set in a dress shop, not outside a dress shop.' Student nodded and changed tack:

Character 2: Alright, we are open.
Character 1: Have you got this dress in a size 12?
Character 2: No.

I pointed out she was saying NO to every offer she made to herself. My student was suddenly able to see it. When she'd taken a moment to think, she said, 'I guess I don't know what is going to happen if I say YES. So I'm saying NO to stop it going somewhere I don't want it to go.'

Bingo.

In this context, NO comes from a fear of the unknown, rather than a desire to say NO. Which is why, in improv, we practise the YES AND mindset to get used to the feeling of not knowing what might happen. That way, we can have a stronger sense of when we need to say NO, rather than fear pushing us to it.

I Don't Like It When People Say NO to Me

I hear you. Luckily, I chose a profession where people say it to me almost every single day.

As a performer, getting used to people saying NO to you is a horrible part of the job.

No, I don't want you to be in my show.

No, you can't audition for this part.

NO, NO, NO, NO!

But my perception of receiving a NO was changed when I went on a workshop at The Actors Centre in Covent Garden many years ago. During a discussion about casting, the teacher said, 'If you have an audition and they reject you, thank them. Because you don't want to work with someone who doesn't think you are right for the part. So be grateful to them for not choosing you, so that you can find the work that fits.' Their NO is a YES to you being you. Don't change for us, they are saying. Continue to be yourself.

When I get a NO from work now, I shrug it off and move on. Ninety-nine per cent of the time, it is not personal.

Someone who isn't into my idea, or the way I interpret a role or even my hair colour* is not a rejection of me, it is an acceptance of who I am and that not being right for what is needed. Separate your SELF from the ideas you present or the trousers you are wearing that day.

People often use Decca, a record label, saying NO to the Beatles as an example of an opportunity lost. The Beatles were auditioning for a recording contract and Decca Records turned them down. These days, it is used as the biggest example of failing to spot talent. But actually, that NO meant that The Beatles met George Martin, who became their long-term producer and collaborator and, it is often said, The Beatles would not have been The Beatles without him[†]. His was the YES they needed to be fully themselves. So thanks, Dick Rowe from Decca. Without you, we wouldn't have had The Beatles.

The Muddle of YES and NO

Is YES and NO really that simple and binary? Yes. And no. There are consequences and perceptions to juggle.

---

* A lot of roles simply come down to hair colour and height. Which is annoying when you walk into a room and the casting director says, 'Oh! You are tall! Not what I was expecting,' even though it says how tall you are on your casting profile. Still in my top ten of 'most annoying things'.

† If you are struggling with these references, have a little internet trip, because Beatles trivia really is part of the international curriculum. Also, it will give you something to talk to old people about.

We might say YES to things because we think that they will lead to other things. It's negotiation, compromise. I will go to see that show with my friend even though I don't particularly like musicals, because I want to see my friend*. I will go for dinner with that client even though I am tired because I need to strengthen this relationship.

Here's an equation for you:

What we want to do + External pressures = Confusion

The most baffling lesson I was ever taught on YES and NO was by my Year 5 teacher at primary school. Brentford Football Club were coming to teach us a special football class. YES. BRENTFORDDDDD! Come on the Bees†! However, there were only two places left in the group. Mrs Buttface (teacher names have been changed to protect identity and to reflect my opinion of them) made me, Manal (quiet girl who sat next to me), Mattius (cheeky boy in class) and Matthew (Barney Rubble lookalike) who had all asked to take part, stand up in the classroom, in front of everyone. She asked us individually, in her very serious teacher voice, 'Will you give up your place so someone else can take it?' and Mattius and I said, 'NO' and Manal and Matthew said, 'YES'. And Manal and Matthew were

---

* This is most of my friends compromising to spend time with me. Sorry not sorry!

† Literally know nothing about football but have worked in local pubs and knew that I could win over the regulars if I occasionally proclaimed my love for the Bees. What a manipulative little barmaid I was. Lots of free drinks though, so . . .

given the places, for, in Mrs Buttface's words, 'Being kind, self-less children'. Mattius and I had to stay in the class with Mrs Buttface while Matthew and Manal went out to play with The Bees. Lesson learned! Don't be selfish, Pippa. Then you will be rewarded.

The following week, we found ourselves in the same position. Brentford were back to lead a football session, but there were only two spots. Ol' Buttface asked the question again and this time, having learnt my lesson, I changed my tack and Manal stuck with her original position, dutifully saying, 'YES'. I would give up my place for someone else. Matthew and Mattius went with, 'NO'. The bids were in and we waited for the results. Manal and I sat in the glow of our good behaviour, ready for our prize. Mrs Buttface said, 'Enjoy the football, Matthew and Mattius.' I was devastated, but mostly confused. We did what she had told us the week before and now we weren't going to get rewarded? Manal and I comforted ourselves by sharing a Penguin bar at break and tried to fathom what had just happened.

If the lesson of week one was, 'be selfless', the lesson of week two was, 'put yourself first'. And so began my complicated relationship with YES and NO. So thank you, Mrs Buttface, because even though you never discussed any of this with us, you set me on a lifelong quest to understand why I say YES or NO. And my conclusion of what Mrs Buttface was trying to teach us is this: choices don't always lead to the result you want – so make sure you really mean the one you are saying out loud. Needless to say I haven't supported Brentford Football Club since.

One of the best things about practising improv is that you are working with imaginary scenarios within which you are having to make these decisions all the time. You practise where YES and NO might take you. You get used to the idea that whenever two or more humans try to communicate their hearts' desires with each other, it is rife with misunderstanding, miscommunication and sometimes misery. When the improv scenes fall apart, it is often because we didn't really listen to what we were saying YES or NO to, and we hadn't given ourselves time to process what we really wanted to say. And that's when it gets messy.

A Messy Yes and No Story

When I was at university, I really fancied this massive jerk. But I couldn't see that he was a jerk, because he was so tall and arrogant (my favourite kind of guy at the time) and I was definitely in self-destruct mode. I was 20, I had broken up with my first proper boyfriend with whom I'd had a pretty unhealthy relationship. I didn't know what I wanted to do with my life, and I had turned to partying to hide the pain.

This guy, the jerk that I was constantly flirting with REFUSED to go out with me. REFUSED. I pursued him for ages and then finally we were drunk enough that we slept together.

My offer was: Let's go out with each other!
His response was: No – I don't want a girlfriend!

Clear NO here from the jerk – did I accept it? Did I squiggly.

My counteroffer was: Come on, let's get drunk and sleep together (and secretly 'then you will fall in love with me').

His response was: No. I don't think you want to just sleep with me – I think you want a boyfriend (although he was a jerk, he was quite astute).

My counteroffer was: No. I just want to sleep with you and won't be upset if you don't call.

His response was: OK. This sounds like a great deal. Let's sleep together then.

And for about ten minutes, I felt like I had won first prize*.

After that night, he never spoke to me again. I tried to snog his best friend to get back at him a few months later and he got his new girlfriend to walk past and laugh at me in a bar one day. So really, no one was a winner. There were a lot of messy offers not being made clearly or truly heard. We both should have walked away, but instead, we had awkward sex in a single bed and it was the worst.

There are lots of things we could have done differently. I could have accepted his first NO because it was an agreement with the truth that was silently there – I wanted him to be my

---

* There was an episode of *Friends* where this situation happened to Phoebe and when I saw it I felt so relieved, because I thought I was an unspeakable human for having behaved in this way and that I deserved to be shamed. So I tell this story because it's a good example, but also because I want you to know we all have to work this stuff out and often that can be painful to go back over. So here is some of my mess to encourage you to investigate yours.

boyfriend, but he knew he just wanted to shag about*. I could have noticed the NO in my belly when the YES came out my mouth. He could have listened to the NO he was saying instead of being seduced by the idea of no-strings sex. Because sometimes there are strings we haven't noticed or choose not to see.

I had mixed up my YES and NO by trying to look cool and breezy when really I was screaming, 'Show me I am loveable!'. He had mixed up his YES and NO by thinking short-term gain over long-term pain. I saw him once in the street a few years back. I was happily carrying a Christmas tree home with my husband. We didn't acknowledge each other. It felt like a scene from the end of a cheesy rom com movie. Satisfyingly, he tripped on the kerb.

Sometimes NO IS A NO

In improv class, unfortunately, there is occasionally the moment when someone takes a scene too far. I have been strangled in a scene where someone wanted to show their character was angry with me. I have stopped a man try to bend a woman over to pretend they were having anal sex, despite this being their first scene together. In these situations, we STOP THE SCENE. We say NO to the offer. The offer is unhelpful, unkind and unproductive.

---

* Hey Mum and Dad! Hope you enjoyed this story! Plenty more where that came from. Strap in!

Once, I was on the Tube and a man sitting next to me started stroking my leg. I couldn't believe it was happening and had that silent terror that unfortunately I know any women reading this book will understand. I leapt up at the next stop and got off the Tube. He followed me to the other end of the platform and then asked if I wanted to be his friend.

'No, I FUCKING DON'T!' I shouted, looking him right in the eye.

He scarpered pretty fast.

It was a clear NO. No one would question that NO, but social pressure meant I didn't scream on the Tube because of the unspoken rule not to make a fuss in public. Also, a knowledge that no one else could see he was touching my leg, so he could just deny it and make me look stupid. It was all about how I might be seen. But him approaching me on the platform gave me permission to shout NO. I was waiting for permission from the situation. But you can give yourself permission. If your gut says something is wrong, if someone is hurting you, if you know you don't want to do this thing, you scream NO as loud as you need to.

Sometimes it takes all our strength to say NO because we are in situations where the status is not in balance, so we have to say YES. Or we have to lose a lot to say NO. And those situations are just awful. We only have to look at the stories from the #MeToo movement to see that. I don't want to ignore my brothers here who also find themselves in situations where to say NO might cost you family, respect or opportunities. Just know that your sisters will have experienced this four-fold. This does not invalidate your experience.

The more we practise saying NO, the easier it becomes. The more we realise that we won't lose everything by saying NO, we can find our allies in situations and become stronger and braver in our NO. When you need a NO, know that it is already there, deep in your belly.

Sometimes, you need to take an extra moment, a breath, to know if you want to say YES or NO. Take that moment. NO is a YES to yourself.

Exercise Corner

For the next week, notice when you say NO. Don't change it, just notice it. Write down any occurrences that stand out. How did it feel to say NO? Was it hard to say? Were there any times you said NO when you meant YES?

When you have that information, think about your relationship with YES and NO. Would you like to say YES more? Do you need more NO in your life?

If you need more YES, make a promise to say YES to one thing this week that your NO wants to protect you from.

If you need more NO, try saying NO to one thing this week. It could be as simple as NO to the dessert menu or NO to a TV show you don't want to watch. NO to a meeting you haven't got time to attend.

If you are happy with the ratio, well done you. Have a cookie!

But only if you want one.

Eye for an Answer

When we are lost in an improv scene – floundering for words, drowning in white noise – we look to our scene partner. We put our focus on them and there the answer is – in their eyes. You realise that you are not alone on the stage. You are working together. You will find the answer together.

The action of focusing on your partner's eyes takes the pressure away from thinking up what to do next. By removing that pressure, what you need to do next comes to you.

Maybe that sounds ridiculous, but I know it to be true.

Try it.

If you don't know what to do, look your partner in the eye.

That is where the answer lies.

Sometimes your partner is you.

Go find a mirror and look yourself in the eye.

Breathe.

You will know what to do.

FOLLOW YOUR OBVIOUS

Did you know that you are creative? It's true. You just have to follow your obvious.

Pick up your phone.

Set two minutes on your timer.

Put down your phone.

Pick up a pen.

Turn each of these shapes into anything other than what they are. If you don't want to draw in your book, take a minute to draw them out on a piece of paper.

Don't think about it too much. Do what your gut tells you. Go!

Great work. How did you do? Take a moment to think about your response to that exercise, while I tell you a story.

I have had dozens of jobs. As a performer, you often do things other than perform to pay the rent. I have worked in pubs and clubs, I have worn an A-board promoting the new location of a Post Office in Hammersmith* and I have worked as security at Wimbledon All England Lawn Tennis Club†. I enjoy doing different things; being plonked in new situations and discovering new worlds within my world.

One of my favourite roles was in market research within product development. I would get paid to spend all day with a load of executives to help them come up with new products for their companies. Mostly, these would be food-related products, which I was happy about as it involved eating a lot of samples. They would tell us about the product they wanted to work with – it could be something generic, like eggs, or it could be more conceptual, such as, 'We need a Valentine's celebration'. This group of young artists and improvisers would then expand on the starter idea, spitballing new ways to look at the product and reinventions of old ideas. I was happy to give my ideas to big conglomerates to turn into megabucks. I was personally never going to make a new

---

* This was not a great lot of fun as mostly people would shout, 'Nice dress!' at me. I used to stand next to this guy wearing a Subway sandwich outfit to feel better. What a cute couple we made.

† True – somewhere, my dad has a horrific picture of me in a security outfit, walking alongside Tim Henman. Little did Tim know, it was not me that was walking next to a legend, but he.

chocolate bar that had a liquid centre – I am no Willy Wonka (although I do love his hat*) – so I loved creating things I wouldn't then have to go and make.

What I also enjoyed about the way in which this company worked, other than the fee (and the Pret sandwich platters which felt so very fancy), was that we simply had to come up with any ideas that occurred to us and say them out loud. The visiting company whose products we were developing had been briefed that if they wanted these creative minds to come up with anything of use, they had to allow us to be free to follow our own logic, rather than try to please the company. To trust that we might get somewhere if we were given space to explore some of the ideas that didn't immediately chime with them. In actuality, these seemingly bonkers ideas could develop into the answer the company was looking for.

Sandwiches

It was a cold, February day. I walked up to a big, grey building in Ladbroke Grove and pressed the buzzer that had a Post-it® Note next to it which read 'Sandwiches'. For yes, today the world's greatest minds (that were free on a Tuesday afternoon and willing to give away their ideas for £80) were thinking about sandwiches. Who thinks about sandwiches? When was the last time you bought a sandwich and thought, 'I wonder

---

* In my mind, there is only one Willy Wonka and that is Gene Wilder. Do not @ me!

how much planning went into this sandwich?' Pre-packaged sandwiches are a six-billion-pound industry in the UK, and on this day, a group of self-identifying creative folk were being entrusted with the job of finding new ways to make them.

Sat around a big table, we were presented with a large selection of sandwiches and asked to feed back about what we thought of them. 'Bit dull,' was one thought. 'Emergency meal,' was another. 'It had better be tastier than if I'd made it myself,' was another. I loved that last thought, as it hadn't occurred to me that we expect so much from a sandwich. These are just sandwiches, but for the consumer to part with at least £3 or more, that sandwich has got to deliver.

The sandwich company was aware that it was in a saturated market, so wanted to know what might catch the eye of the consumer. I piped up with the idea that maybe, if we want them to be as good as if we made them, they should look a bit like we did. Someone else YES AND-ed my thought and suggested they should be packaged like when you were a kid. I remembered a café in Victoria station that sold cheese and pickle rolls wrapped in cling-film. They were the tastiest sandwiches in existence, and not just because they had amazing ingredients, but because they looked like you brought them from home. The sandwich fan saw them and was transported to packed lunches of their childhood, hungrily opening their lunch box to see what their mum* had put in there.

---

* I recognise not everyone's packed lunch will have been made by their mum, but there is no way my dad could have been entrusted to make me a packed lunch. He once had to cook me an egg and all I remember is crying and saying, 'It doesn't taste right'.

This thought led us to talk about how nice it was when you were a kid and maybe your sandwiches were cut into squares or triangles*. Someone noted that it would be nice if you could get sandwiches cut into two rectangles instead of the usual triangles. Voices started talking enthusiastically about going to a posh afternoon tea and getting different flavours of sandwiches, but cut really small. Someone spoke of the brown paper bag that you get if you buy your sandwich from a deli instead of a supermarket. All of these thoughts came from free associating around the topic of sandwiches.

Free Association

'Free association' is a term and method the psychoanalyst Freud used to explore the connections the individual makes without being led by the therapist. The patient explores their own connections and ideas, allowing them to reveal the way their own mind works. By allowing the patient to work in this way, without judgement or immediate analysis, they can find their own logic of association. In other words, they can follow their obvious, and then consider how they made those connections at a later date.

In improvisation, games involving free association are used to unlock the creative mind so that the performer is not worrying about saying the 'right' thing, but rather revealing the thoughts and ideas that come to them in the moment. I

---

* Hugely divisive topic – some strong opinions as to whether triangles or squares are better.

remember a workshop I once ran with a group of women who were experiencing homelessness. We were playing a free association game and they were giving each other words to free associate from. One participant turned to another and said, 'Place you might sleep', from which her partner listed, 'Cardboard, sleeping bag, tunnel, someone's floor, sofa, hostel, bed.' As someone who has never experienced homelessness, it was shocking to me that it took this woman six items before she spoke of a bed. What a different world I had been let into. How different her list would have been if I had told her, 'I will be judging each of your answers to be sure you get it right.' Her obvious was revealed, and led us to truthful work based in her truth, rather than enforcing my life experience upon her creativity.

Back in Ladbroke Grove, the sandwich people were very interested in these sandwich links to childhood and to fancy high teas. In how the way in which the sandwiches were packed might impact our associations with sandwiches of the past and memories of lunchboxes long gone. We then talked about flavours. We all went for 70s classics – prawn cocktail, cheese and pickle – and got into some quite heated conversations about Coronation chicken*. Then it was time to go. We collected our £80 (cash, baby!) and left the room.

Now, I can't take credit for the sandwiches that then appeared on the shelves, but if you walk into any supermarket that sells pre-packaged sandwiches, you will now see the high

---

* I am pro Coronation chicken, which I hope won't make it hard for you to continue reading my book. Please separate the artist from their preferred sandwich fillings.

end sandwiches in a brown paper bag (cut into rectangles, not triangles, I might add) and also small selections of little triangle sandwiches of different 1970s flavours. Whenever I buy one of these products I whisper to the cashier conspiratorially, 'I helped come up with these.' And they tend to look at me like they wish I would stop speaking to them. But I can't help being thrilled to know that my obvious is in that sandwich.

Creativity is not often associated with sandwiches, but it is the imagination that is the gateway to change. William Blake, the great poet/artist, said in *The Marriage of Heaven and Hell*, 'What is now proved was once only imagin'd'. Everything we take for granted was once just a little grain of obvious in someone's mind.

Following Your Obvious Can Lead to Revolution

The wheelie bin is a great physical example of someone following their obvious, because when people talk about wheelie bins, they often say, 'Why didn't I think of that? It's so obvious!' Invented by Frank Rotherham Mouldings in 1968, the wheelie bin was originally just used in a factory to take rubbish from one end to another. However, after being spied by a health and safety officer, it was thought to be a great solution to back problems the UK's refuse workers were suffering after lugging the old big metal bins around. Backs were saved by Frank's obvious.

The first women's refuge was set up in 1971 in Chiswick, when it became obvious to Erin Pizzey and Anne Ashby of

Chiswick Women's Aid that women needed a safe haven to escape from domestic abuse. At that time, there was no law against marital rape in the UK, and women could not apply for a mortgage, meaning that women in abusive relationships were often trapped within a marriage with nowhere to go. By following their obvious, hundreds of women's lives have been saved and the charity Refuge continues Pizzey and Ashby's incredible bravery in following their obvious.

Indeed, revolutions have been started by people following their obvious. Take Rosa Parks: she refused to give up her seat to a white man in a segregated bus. She wasn't following the law, she was following her obvious – that a Black woman should not have to give up her seat simply because a white man was present. This law-defying act led to other people seeing her perspective and, following the Montgomery Bus Boycott of 1955–56, bus segregation (where Black people would have to sit at the back of the bus and white people at the front) was deemed unconstitutional, making her obvious the new law. By following our obvious we can engage people in a different perspective, a new prism which illuminates a situation in a new light.

Smaller Ways to Follow Your Obvious

Following your obvious does not have to lead to a new way of carrying refuse, but it can do. It doesn't have to lead to revolutions, but it can do. Following your obvious might simply create a new way of doing things at work or influence the choices when cooking a meal. How many times have you followed a recipe and thought, 'Oh, I wouldn't do it like that'? Whatever the outcome, following your obvious or exploring someone else's obvious with them will expand your creativity and the directions that your logic can take you.

Let's go back to those pictures. Below, you'll see what I drew and I want you to look at the similarities and differences between these and your own creations. I am not an artist in any way – my drawings are not the 'right' drawings – this is simply a way to illustrate how the same stimulus can create vastly different responses.

Where can you see our brains going in the same direction?

And where can you see us going in completely different ones?

No More Shaming the Obvious

Being obvious has been an insult for so long, it has stopped us being willing to say our thoughts out loud. How many times have you said or heard, 'This might be too obvious, but . . .' as a protection before someone gives their idea? What is obvious to me is not necessarily what is obvious to you. These illustrations are a case in point. Maybe you and I both made the square into a house. But you put the chimney on the other side. Maybe you turned it into something completely different, like a tunnel or a square cartoon character, a sandwich or a box of cereal. Whatever you did, that was your obvious.

When we are improvising, when we are given a scenario and go on stage with what we have to hand, we have to be able to trust our obvious. To follow through our thoughts without letting any brain funk get in the way. Trust where your imagination wants you to go – otherwise, you'll just remain sitting with the shapes at the beginning of the chapter, and that is a far less satisfying feeling than releasing your ideas out into the world. Obvious doesn't make it less original, for it is your personal twist on being obvious.

What if What I Say Really Is Too Obvious?

If it really seems too obvious, then YES AND it. Too obvious just means we are repeating the first idea again. There is no harm in it – we just can't finish there. Join the two improv principles together. Follow your obvious and YES AND yourself.

Go back to the pictures at the top of the chapter. Let's take the triangle shape. Let's have an imaginary thought process about what we could turn it into.

It's a triangle (obvious).

Yes – and it has been sliced from a pyramid (my obvious).

Yes – and it has hieroglyphics on it (detailed obvious).

And the hieroglyphics say BE OBVIOUS.

Don't be scared of speaking your obvious. It might be the key to creating something else – a piece of the jigsaw, whether that is problem-solving at work, discussing what to do at the weekend with the kids, or coming up with new, fantastic sandwiches.

Be obvious. Your obvious.

Exercise Corner

SOLO

Free writing is a great way to tap into the subconscious and follow your obvious. Set a timer for three minutes and start writing, inspired by any of the following words:

Home

Love

Passion

Rage

Dreams

You can use a pen and paper or a computer – the only rule is that you cannot correct anything. You will just write following where the words take you – wherever your obvious wants you to go. It may not make complete sense, what you write – in fact, some of it will be nonsensical, but keep going until your timer buzzes that the three minutes are up. Practising free writing is a great outlet for subconscious thought and seeing where your brain takes you when it isn't restricted by structure or outcome.

Read back over what you have written. Has anything come up that you want to explore more? An idea or thought that you weren't aware of? Set the timer again and use this idea or thought as your starting point. See where your obvious takes you.

IN A PAIR

Endless Box

This is a classic improvisation game about exercising those imagination muscles to show just how much there is in your noggin to play with. One of the things that makes me saddest is how many people tell me they are not creative because they work in accounts or they were told at school they couldn't do art GCSE*. We all have creativity in us – but if we haven't explored it since primary school, it might take a bit of time to coax out.

Sit on a chair opposite each other and imagine there is a big cardboard box in front of you. This exercise is one of free association, so be sure not to judge what you find.

Simply be curious.

One of you reaches into the box and pulls out imaginary items. Literally put your arm out – as if you were putting it into a box – and pull out some things. Really see them in your hand. Show their shape in how you grip them. Enjoy seeing them. Whatever you see, you are right.

The second person's job is simply to say 'YES' to whatever you say the thing is.

---

* This happened to me when I was 15 and I took it as a sign that I was not creative. Actually, I was not scholastically able to draw a replica of my friend Bea's face in a way that would allow my school to get further in the league tables. And that was probably true. The league tables win again! Creativity and ability to do a good drawing are very different things. Please allow your mind to separate them.

Example:

Person 1: A cat!
Person 2: Yes!
Person 1: A marshmallow.
Person 2: Yes!
Person 1: A machine gun.
Person 2: Yes!
Person 1: Death.
Person 2: Yes indeed!

I have included in this example some unpleasant things (machine gun, death) that appeared out of the imaginary box for me. Don't be frightened of what you pull out. Often, if you have not had a creative outlet for a while, sexual and dark themes emerge. These are things social norms require us to be careful about mentioning in public. It is no surprise then that at the first opportunity to free associate, they emerge. I have had students cover their mouths when words have come out, as if trying to shove them back in; scared of what has been revealed of them.

They are just things – thoughts that are in your head, as they are in all of us. As long as you don't pull out an actual gun and shoot anyone, an imaginary one does no harm. That is why the YES person is there – to allow you to accept everything that comes out of your mind. Once we are comfortable with the depth of our imagination, we can stop self-censoring when it does not serve us. We begin to accept all of us, even the dark or complicated bits.

If you find this exercise easy, go faster.

Try not to say, 'Ummmm,' or, 'Errrrr,' before naming the object. This is stalling for time so you can think of the item, rather than discover it.

You are aiming to get to the point where you are surprising yourself with what you are pulling out of the box. At that point, we are allowing our intuition to take over our intellect and stretching our brain in a way that day-to-day activity does not.

This is not about being clever or sensible. It is about being obvious.

LOSE CONTROL.
GAIN PERSPECTIVE.

I got married in 2010 to an incredibly kind, generous man. Thank you, yes, I am very lucky. Yet in the run up to our big day, this man, normally so relaxed and calm, turned into the biggest control freak you have ever witnessed. He wanted everything to be perfect, which meant he needed to be in charge of every single detail. And I mean every single detail; never before in my life had I seen anyone measure the distance between the lettering on an invitation.

'It's supposed to be 0.2mm!' he cried, and then rang up the printers to complain.

Forget Bridezilla – this was Groomzilla. I wasn't allowed to do anything without running it past him first, and whilst I didn't really mind (it meant I could have a very relaxing wedding experience) I could see there was potential for this to all go a bit wrong.

I suppose I knew it was a little out of hand when we couldn't find the right lamps for the table centrepieces at the reception (flowers deemed 'too obvious*') and so he declared, 'I shall make fifteen lamps myself!'

---

* Should have read him that last chapter.

Let me explain. These weren't just little flouncy paper lamps, but intricately crafted working lamps with bulb fittings and everything. Patterns cut into thick card, sealed with a glue gun and attached to individual electric lights. The kind of thing they make on craft shows and you think, 'Who the hell is going to actually make that?' My husband, that is who.

'Are you sure?' I replied, thinking even the most robust lamp designer would struggle to make fifteen individual lamps in two weeks, let alone an IT Consultant with only his evenings free and several other items on his to-do list. 'Yes, it is the only solution.' I offered to help, but my card-cutting skills were deemed not worthy and so I left him to it. After all, if he knew what he wanted to do, why not let him get on with it?

My brother and sister-in-law, Sam and Suzie, gave me a call the week before the wedding and asked if they should come down from Birmingham a day or two early to help with the preparations.

'No!' Groomzilla declared. 'Everything is in hand.' I looked at the craft card, light fittings and patterns, piled up in the corner. 'Are you sure? Remember, I am spending the day before the wedding with Mum, so I won't be here to help.' Groomzilla was adamant he could do it all, and so Sam and Suzie put down the phone, warm in the glow at having made a lovely offer and not having to do any hard labour.

The day before the wedding arrived, and I was getting ready to leave for Mum's. I opened the living room door and there was Groomzilla, surrounded by half-made lamps, looking completely stressed out of his mind, holding a Stanley knife in one hand and his head in the other.

'Are you alright?' I asked, knowing he wasn't.

'I just have so much to do. I haven't collected my suit, I need to meet my best man at six o' clock and there are twelve more lamps to be made.' he whimpered.

'Do you want me to stay and help you?'

'No. You're supposed to spend the day with your Mum,' he replied. Which was true.

'Do you want me to call Sam and Suzie and see if they can still come down early?' I asked. He sat still for a moment and then whispered, 'Yes.'

Luckily, Sam and Suzie had planned for such an eventuality and jumped in their car. I called Mum and told her I would be there a bit later and went to collect Groomzilla's suit. Sam and Suzie were with him by lunchtime, constructing the last 12 intricately-patterned lamps. They cut and glued and laughed about all the things that didn't quite work out at their wedding. Groomzilla had some company to keep him sane, managed to meet his best man, and best of all, the lamps got made. Sure, they weren't exactly how Groomzilla had imagined them – they now had a bit of Sam and Suzie baked in – but they were beautiful. Groomzilla disappeared and Calum returned (for that is his real name). And even though the printing company didn't quite rectify all the measurements and the caterer got confused about how many vegetarians there were, it was a beautiful day, and everyone commented on the lovely lamps. By relinquishing even just the tiniest bit of control, Calum was able to enjoy the process, instead of trying to make it perfect. Which meant it *was* perfect, because how can anything be perfect if you aren't enjoying it?

I Just Want to Make It Perfect

Being good at organising things, and knowing who needs to do what to make X happen – these strengths around organisation and group management are great. These are useful skills to have but only when applied with *humility* and *flexibility*. Without these additional traits, being a great team leader can slide into being controlling and dictatorial. In fact, to find ourselves in the sweet spot for any of our strengths to flourish, they usually need to be used in combination with a seemingly contradictory strength. Control and agility, generosity and boundaries, being in the moment whilst seeing the bigger picture.

Getting things finished is not the only consideration when working on a project. You want everyone in the process to feel they contributed – that they had a part in making something happen. If people are just following your orders – being told how to do what you ask them to do – then how can they invest in the project at all? They are a worker bee without the camaraderie. Even with the mistakes Calum had so feared, the wedding still happened. Even when things went wrong, we had the skills to find solutions. You could even say that those mistakes are what made us. Working through the Great Lamp Crisis of 2010 meant we had to pull together. Calum found not being in control a tiny bit easier, and Sam and Suzie learned the intricate skills of table illumination.

Truth Bomb

It is impossible to control everything in your life.

Let that sink in. Take a moment to think about the truth of that.

We are taught that life is linear. We can live our lives to our own designed (or for those in some faiths, predesigned) path, and if we make the right choices, we will win at life. That if we work hard and get qualifications, we can get the job we want and we will live happily ever after. Life is not a straight line. It is a tangle of tangents and pathways which, if we were presented with them at the beginning of our time on Earth, we would say, 'No thank you!' and climb back into our mother's womb. We have to learn to be at one with not being able to control every aspect of our life. All we can do is work on our inner selves and our internal world so that we are able to respond to what the external world throws at us.

This idea that we must recognise what we can control – and also what we cannot – goes all the way back to the Greek philosophers. It was Epictetus who said: 'Some things are not up to us'. Can't put it plainer than that. We have limited control over what happens in the world, but we do have control over our thoughts and beliefs. Too often we try to control something external that is not in our control, and this makes us feel wretched*.

You Never Expect the Unexpected

When Covid-19 spread across the world in 2020, how many of us had our lives turned upside down? Suddenly, parents were working from home and having to home-school. We were confined to our tiny flats. Jobs were lost. Opportunities we had lined up disappeared. People got sick. Operations were cancelled. People died. Being controlling is a response to fear of the unknown. In our quest to plan for every eventuality, we think we can ensure that nothing can go wrong. Yet when we are at the mercy of so many variables, including pandemics, how can it ever be possible to control the way life pans out?

And yet, whilst there was darkness, there was also light. Families found they were spending more time with each other without the work commute. Communities started reconnecting with each other as they offered to help their neighbours with shopping. People were cooking more and eating together. They realised they wanted connection over accolades. By

---

* I feel both a relief and an amazement that we are still struggling with the same issues that they were back in Greece, thousands of years ago. An Ancient Greek theatre producer pulling their hair out because someone hasn't ordered the right number of togas for the latest production of *Oedipus Rex*.

having time to stop and reflect, something they would not have had without a sudden restriction of circumstances, people made choices about what changes they wanted to make to the way they were living. Control was lost for a while, but perhaps purpose was found.

It doesn't take a pandemic for our lives to be thrown into disarray. It could be job loss, a friend letting us down, a bus not arriving on time, a partner cheating on us – the list goes on and on with things that can or might happen. If you tried to control all the possible outcomes of every possible event, you would go mad. So, in truth, the only thing we can control is our response to things that are not in our control. We can scream and cry at the injustice of it all and we can mourn what might have been, but then we have to pick ourselves up and decide what to do next.

Trying to Control It All

How many of us try to put measures in place to limit the chaos of everyday? Leaving nothing up to chance, we make demands on our partners to be perfect, our families to never let us down and our children to behave like automatons. Not going to happen. If there is ever anyone who can teach us how to let go of control, it is children.

The author and journalist Lucy Cavendish wrote an article about spending a week having given her children permission to take complete control of how she ran the household. What to eat, what activities they got up to, what time they went to bed. This was a great experiment in relinquishing control, and I love what Lucy says in her conclusion. Having also been a self-confessed control freak and often saying 'NO' to her children's requests because they would lead to mess or unpredictable results, she noticed: 'The hassle of clearing up the kitchen after they have made a cake is nothing compared to the joy I feel when I hear them laughing so freely. They just wanted to have fun, to laugh more; to not have every request quashed by a negative.'

To embrace life, we have to give up control. We cannot have deep, nuanced relationships with other people if we have decided exactly how we want them to be, rather than responding to how they are. By letting other people take control of their part in any process, be that dealing with a family crisis or running a business meeting, we will expand our experience of the world.

Control in Improv

Controlling scenes is a common issue in improv, particularly when first starting. A new improviser is entering an unknown entity, feeling vulnerable in front of her classmates. It is no wonder her first reflex is to try and make it safer for herself. Imagine a group of improvisers are asked to take the stage. One improviser steps forward into the space and declares:

'I am here in this bar as the mayor of Tennessee and I am banning all music.'

Strong start – we know where we are (a bar), who they are (the mayor), and what they are doing (banning the music). A couple more improvisers take to the stage, as drinkers in this here bar, but before they have a chance to add anything else, the mayor speaks again:

'I know what you are thinking – you want me to lose the next election. Well, I don't think so.'

Again, the improvisers take a breath to respond to the mayor, but the mayor does not leave space for them and continues:

'Don't point that gun at me, Mary Sue!'

The improvisers look surprised – they weren't pointing a gun – they were calmly drinking an imaginary beer. They know they need to continue with the scene, so even though they feel like the scene is being dictated to them, one of the performers accepts that they are Mary Sue to YES AND the Mayor and turns their imaginary beer into an imaginary gun.

Mary Sue goes to reply but the mayor acts as if he has been shot:

'How could you, Mary Sue? I thought we were friends?'

While the other improvisers look at each other, not sure what just happened, the improviser playing the mayor slides to the floor, performing a magnificent death. The scene was great fun to the crowd, but the improvisers, other than the mayor, feel disgruntled.

Why are they disgruntled? The performer playing the mayor has not allowed anyone else to contribute to the scene. They most likely think they are being an excellent improviser, bringing all of the information (Who What Where) so that no one else has to worry about it. But by playing in this way, the mayor is telling the other improvisers, 'I don't trust you. I don't believe in you to make a good scene,' and simultaneously, 'I don't trust myself to be able to follow where you might lead me.'

If we were in a workshop, I would ask this improviser to notice what they were doing. Can they see that they are imposing not just an identity on everyone, but also everyone's responses to the situation? Can they see that they have set down all the rules for the scene? Can they see they have not left space for anyone to steer the scene anywhere other than where they have demanded? Simply by noticing this behaviour, the improviser can reflect on why. Then we can play the scene again and see if the same behaviour continues. If it does, we can work on letting go of control. I can tell them to enter as the mayor, but say that they aren't allowed to say anything. We can see how they feel when they have no control over the scene. We can make them play the scene again, but I will then shout directions that stop them being able to plan their next move. 'Start dancing!' or 'Tell everyone a joke.' Improv is a space where we can notice and work on these tendencies in a scenario where there are no consequences other than learning. It is a safe place to explore our weaknesses.

Why Do I Like Controlling Everything?

Control is a defence against the fear of uncertainty, and if there is one place that you need to be OK with uncertainty, it is improv. When I am working with students on scene work, I encourage them to embrace 'folding their ideas'. This comes from poker, where you might fold a weaker hand of cards when someone plays a stronger one. In improvisation, it is not that your offer is necessarily weaker, just that it is no longer relevant. You come into a scene thinking it's going to be a courtroom but someone else turns it into a car dealership. You have to fold your idea. It is not going to be a courtroom. Throw it away. No matter how fabulous you thought that courtroom scene was going to be, get involved in the car dealership. You start walking onto the stage thinking you are a slow, old woman but another improviser names you Monsoon, the Dragon King. You have to fold your idea and find a reason that the Dragon King walks in this particular way. So often we come on stage with an idea that we have to discard because it is no longer appropriate for the scene that is playing out. In five seconds it has gone from a possibility to an impossibility, and, as improvisers, we need to be OK with that. If you want to be a great improviser, you have to let it go. If you want to be a team player, you have to follow the flow of the team, rather than your own agenda. If you want to be a good partner, you have to let your loved one fill the dishwasher however they wish*.

---

* Even if it is undeniably wrong.

Getting Things Right

There is rarely one right way to do anything*. You ask different people how they think they could make public transport better in your area: one person might write to their MP to demand more bus shelters whilst another might call a community meeting or make a Facebook group called 'Bus Blues'.

You ask a politician how to run the country. They will say, 'Raise the taxes!' or, 'Lower the taxes!' or, 'I don't know – whatever you think'. You only have to look at Twitter to see how much we don't agree on this one. Which is why 'getting it right' is an impossible challenge for us, because we don't know if we have got 'it' right until 'it' is done. We can question choices our colleagues make along the way but until the work is done, we cannot know if we hit the 'right way'. So rather than controlling things to get them 'right', be open to getting it done, differently.

The improviser in the scene described before isn't wrong for coming on as the mayor, or suggesting there is a ban on music, but they are being short-sighted. They aren't allowing for the possibility that there might be something richer, deeper, other, that can be created collaboratively, rather than following a single vision to a pre-planned end point. When we decide that there is only one way, we cut off hundreds of tiny possibilities that are there, hidden behind the doors of your collaborators' minds. Rather than getting from A to B, we

---

* Except maybe wiring a plug. Please don't improvise that.

might have got to Q. If we are fixated on B, we never get to visit the rest of the alphabet.

Loosen up Just a Little

There is nothing wrong with wanting to do things well – planning events meticulously and making sure you have every element covered. It is when the wish to control outcomes compromises our ability to work in relation to others that we are losing out. Complete control stops any ability to adapt and be creative in the moment.

It is hard to let go of control – it might even be traumatic. It takes a while for these changes to settle in. Start small. Let the kids have ketchup whilst wearing a white T-shirt. Let your colleague organise the next team meeting. Don't weigh out your Cheerios. Whatever area it is that you see control turning your knuckles white, loosen your grip a smidge and see what happens. You'll see how people can approach the same thing, but differently. You can observe their 'obvious' and get a slice of how someone else sees the world. And sure, things might break, and plans might have to adapt*, but new worlds will open up, and collaborators will benefit from seeing you stop trying to control everything and start trying to trust them and their impulses.

---

* Adapting is just tweaking the plan. So, if it helps, you can still say it was your original plan, but tweaked a bit. Like when bands tour with none of the original members.

Letting Go of Control in Action

Big Local is one of the most amazing examples of giving up control I have ever seen. The charity has awarded £1 million to 150 local communities *each* to do with whatever they wish. It sounds absolutely bonkers, but through this initiative, communities that have found themselves falling through the cracks or being ignored by society have made great change for themselves. Big Local aims to empower communities to make their own decisions, rather than enforce upon them what they must use the money for. This means that the money has been used for more obvious community activities like arranging for a minibus to take people without their own mode of transport out and about, and creating a zombie film that looked at problems of regeneration and intergenerational identity within a neighbourhood. It is not like any other funding scheme I have heard of. Matt Leach, the Chief Executive of Local Trust who created this project, said: 'Our approach to outcomes was to emphasise that the development of trust, confidence, skills and partnerships at a local level was just as important as the sorts of hard project-based outcomes that can dominate traditional funding.'

The communities are supported in the development and delivery of their community plans, but all support is delivered with a light touch. Big Local also realised that with different communities having different needs, they couldn't use one set of metrics to measure if the individual projects could be deemed a success. This is a huge giving up of control

– working with each community to see how well their project is going, rather than telling them that they have to achieve a generic metric goal (e.g. number of people helped, distribution of funds per head) that might not be applicable to the way in which they were using the money.

When Matt Leach talks about the development of trust and confidence, we can see how dominant control methods will inhibit this. By Big Local trusting the communities, they in turn begin to trust Big Local (this is some feat, as traditionally these communities have been ignored by the authorities, so trust is a big ask) and as the work starts to unfold, so the confidence grows. Letting go of control might just be the way for people to trust you, and themselves, more. Which, in turn, will enable you to trust yourself.

Expand your trust in others to expand the trust in your own responses.

Because the only thing you can actually control, is you.

Exercise Corner

SOLO

Start breaking your routine, friend. If you have controlling tendencies, you probably have things you like to do in a certain order. Some of this will be conscious, other parts subconscious. For example – you brush your teeth, then wash your face and then put on your PJs at night. You always take a certain route to your friend's house. You eat the same thing for breakfast.

Do it differently. A tiny change. Put your PJs on first. Turn left instead of right. Have toast instead of muesli. Whatever it is, break it just a tiny bit to see a) how you feel and b) how the thing still gets done. By playing with the little ways we control our lives, we can start to believe that life will always find a way.

IN A PAIR

New Choice

This game is so brilliant for exorcising your control freak. An exorcise exercise!

You will need someone else to play this game with, so choose someone you trust who loves you and all your control freakiness.

Imagine you are giving a speech at the wedding of a friend. They can be real or made up. Speak in full sentences which end clearly. For example:

Person 1: Mabel is my best friend in the whole world. I have loved her since we first met in the playground. We swung on the swings and I knew we would be friends for life.

Your partner is going to interrupt you at the end of some sentences with the phrase 'New Choice' and you will immediately have to come up with a new idea. For example:

Person 1: Mabel is my best friend in the whole world.
Person 2: New Choice!
Person 1: Mabel is my enemy and I hate her.
Person 2: New Choice!
Person 1: Mabel is the light of my life and I wish I had married her.

Person 1 must now continue with this being the 'truth' of the scene. Your previous idea is gone and you must build from here. Person 2 – make sure you allow the idea to develop a little before you put the New Choice in, so it tips the balance just when Person 1 thinks they are plain sailing to the end.

Person 1: Mabel is the light of my life and I wish to marry her. On a beach at sunset. We'll put flowers in her hair and I will wear a tuxedo.
Person 2: New Choice!
Person 1: I will wear a bra.
Person 2: New Choice!
Person 1: I will wear nothing. It's a nudist beach.
Person 2: *Giggles and lets the speech continue ...*

This is fantastic practice for switching direction just when you think you know where you are going, and being frustrated when someone wants you to go down a different path. We are furious with our partner because we thought we knew what was going to happen, but we soon find a new path and are able to accept that our 'right' way is not the only way. There is always a new choice that can be made.

Time
for
a
dance
break

We've covered a lot so far. To make sure that it's going in, take a moment to look back and see what you remember. Remind yourself of things that have really spoken to you.

Perhaps you really noticed how you use the word 'Yes' or how much you like to be in control all the time. Maybe there was something you disagreed with. Imagine I am there in the room with you and talk me through your thoughts.

Feel free to flick back through the chapters and remind yourself of what you have read so far. Very few people can remember everything they just read. Take a pen and paper or record yourself a voice note about what has grabbed your attention so far.

And now, move your body. Wave your arms or get out of your chair. Wiggle your toes or do some fast eyebrow action. Anything that takes you out of your head and into your body.

Maybe put on some music and move about to tunes – whether that's Lizzo or Gilbert and Sullivan. Heck, put them both on.

Just dance.

**Keep
on
Dancing!**

LISTEN TO YOUR BODY

I am making an assumption that you have a body. It's the kind of person I am – all sweeping generalisations. Maybe you love your body, maybe your body is frustrating to you or maybe you never even give it a second thought, because you are too busy covering it in high fashion and painting the town. Well, for this chapter, I would like you to take a moment to acknowledge your body. Our thoughts are linked to our bodies. Our emotions are linked to our bodies. Every reaction we have, we feel it, inside us. That is thanks to these lumpy, lanky, chubby, skinny, bumpy, beautiful slabs of meat that keep us alive.

I haven't always appreciated my body. I am a 38-year-old woman who grew up in West London in the 90s. I went to an all-girl school where hating on yourself was an extracurricular activity. We would punish our bodies for being soft, warm and inviting and try to shape them into planks of wood. Hard and flat. We begged our thighs to stop jiggling when we ran. When our bodies failed us, we bonded in the misery of having one. 'Oh, it is so hard, I just want to be thin!' We shamed each other for not looking like Barbie® or Kate Moss, and enjoyed the drama of it all. It makes me sad to think of it now. Our bodies were separate to our souls. If we could have carved our limbs into the right shape, we would have.

It wasn't always this way. I have this one memory of pretending to be a tree blowing in the wind in my primary school hall, leaping around in my PE kit (vest, pants and plimsolls, please), happily moving my body; not questioning its size or validity. Then a second memory of a dance class at high school, where we had to wear leotards and make up a dance to 'The Rime of the Ancient Mariner'*. Suddenly, I was trying to hide my hips and felt awkward moving in front of my peers. If you wish to destroy one hundred 13-year-old girls at once, put them in leotards and make them dance to old poetry in front of the whole school.

It took a long time to realise hating on my body was not going to get me anywhere. Even if you want to change your body, you have to love your body first. Your body is what lets you breathe in and out. Your body gets you from A to B. Your body takes you to amazing locations and feels the sun. Your body knows when you are sick and tells you to go to bed. Your body knows when you have had too much to drink and makes you vomit in a car park. Your body is as clever as you but perhaps a little wiser. Even if you don't have the body you wish you did, I beg of you, love that body.

---

* 'The Rime of the Ancient Mariner' is a poem by the poet Coleridge which is, I am sure, very good, but not 100 per cent on brand for the average 13-year-old who has been forced to prance in public.

Noticing Our Bodies

Where are you right now? What is your body doing? Take a moment to notice how you are sat/stood/curled up. If you are in a public place, take a moment to look around. What are other people doing with their bodies? How are they holding themselves? What can you see that is a conscious choice and what can you see that is unconscious? Perhaps someone is listening to music and tapping their foot, unaware. Perhaps two people are having a business meeting but appear as if they are performing for each other. If you are in a café, perhaps the server is staring at a customer with a blank expression and then suddenly smiles, remembering their training.

I often feel that we have forgotten our bodies. Most of us don't have to ask much of them as the majority of jobs ask us to sit at our desks (e.g. office work or taxi-driving) or stand for hours at a time (e.g. retail or security work). It is suggested that in the UK, we spend on average nine hours sitting a day, which means that if we add in the hours we are asleep, there is not a whole lot of moving our body going on. The NHS cite this little piece of research:

The link between illness and sitting first emerged in the 1950s, when researchers found double decker bus drivers were twice as likely to have heart attacks as their bus conductor colleagues. The drivers sat for 90 per cent of their shifts, the conductors climbed about 600 stairs each working day.

It is not just the health aspect of sitting that is problematic. This sitting allows us to disconnect from our bodies as part of us. We stop paying attention to what our body is saying, even when that is: 'Please move me'. In addition, a lot of us have become less practiced in communicating in person, as the majority of our communication has slowly moved from in-person over to email, WhatsApp and Zoom. We have become thought- and word-focused; 'in our heads' rather than noticing the whole.

This disconnect from our bodies, our lack of noticing what our bodies are saying, is particularly problematic in improv, when performers don't realise they are making offers to themselves, before they have even opened their mouths. A performer unconsciously shakes their head as they walk on the stage. The audience sees something which the improviser has not noticed themselves. There is a mis-step in performer/audience communication, which, in such an immediate form as improv, is not optimal. So how often are we making these unconscious offers in real life? Physically telling our date that we don't want to be there, though our words say something else? Giving off vibes of frustration while trying to organise a dysfunctional team? If we can get a hang on these unconscious offers from our bodies, we can improve our communication. I love what director and improvisation practitioner Viola Spolin says in her book, *Improvisation for the Theatre*:

A player's knowledge that he or she is one unified organism arrives when the whole body, from head to toe, functions as one unit in a life response. The whole body is a vehicle of expression and must develop as a sensitive instrument for perceiving, making contact and communicating.

Reconnecting With Your Body

Before we perform an improv show (indeed, any kind of performance) it is really important that we warm up physically and reconnect with our bodies. We may well have been sat down all day, so we need to be able to check in with any tensions in the body, any emotions hanging around, any physical pain we might need to address. Acknowledge it, address it, and then shake it off, as Taylor would say, or breathe it out, as your doctor would say, before we go on stage and create something new, together.

One of the best ways to reconnect with our bodies comes from the mindfulness movement and is called the body scan. In its simplest form you can sit or lie down, close your eyes and put your attention on your feet. Then move that attention, slowly, up your body, noticing every sensation in every part of you. Perhaps you will feel muscle soreness, as in physical pain, or you might receive a functional message, as in, 'I am hungry', or you may notice an emotion 'There is sadness in my chest'. All of this should be done without judgement and, instead, with curiosity. The more regularly we connect with our bodies, the more easily we receive the information it is sending. Doing a regular body scan will help solidify that relationship so that you are able to feel what your body is saying, in an instant.

What Do You Mean,
Feel What My Body is Saying?

Think of the last time you told a lie (no judgement, friend, we all do it). Perhaps you pretended you had a meeting when you just didn't want to meet someone, or you told your friend you liked their new hair when you didn't. Take a moment to remember how it felt. Did your body fight you in that moment? Your temperature might have raised, or perhaps there was a shake in your voice or you blushed. That is your body disagreeing with the words coming out of your mouth. Most of us believe that lying is dishonest, so even when we are telling a lie to spare someone's feelings, it is almost impossible to cover it up completely.

We notice certain physiological sensations when we lie. It is incredible how much our bodies know. Even when we have made an active choice to deceive someone, most people (psychopath's excepted, perhaps) find that we can't control our own body's reaction sending us messages. We know, when we lie, we have to keep those 'vibrations' under control. If we start controlling those responses regularly, we start altering our ability to hear what our bodies are saying. We start to believe the controlled message, rather than the actual message.

We can feel when someone isn't telling us the truth, but we might not be able to put our finger on how we know. When your girlfriend says that she loves the gift, but you don't believe her, somehow. When your boss says she 'Just can't think why you weren't on the list for the promotion,' but it doesn't ring true. It is not that there are specific individual activities that we do when we are telling a fib, but rather when we are being inauthentic, our non-verbal and verbal behaviours misalign. Our words do not match our actions or even our energy. Something feels 'off'. That 'off' feeling when you lie is you having a connection with your body. The deeper your connection, the more you will be able to receive these non-verbal clues from yourself and your interactions with others. The more open and aware you are of your own subconscious offers, the more able you will be to pick up the subconscious offers of your friends, family and colleagues.

In improv training, once we have installed the body scan as a regular practice, we can really start to notice all those unconscious, misaligned external offers we have been making, without even realising. The same is true in life. I would highly recommend installing the body scan in your day to day activities. Put the kettle on in the morning and use the time for the water to boil to check in with your head, shoulders, knees and toes*.

Our Bodies in the Physical Space

In improv, we have to notice everything that is happening in each interaction, not just words. What occurs in the silence may even be the most interesting. What can we sense our

---

* No – you don't have to sing the song.

partner is telling us? I am not talking about learning tricks to figure out the subtext, we are working on being in the moment; fully present in our bodies so we can notice everything non-verbal that is happening. This enables us to respond truthfully, rather than how we think we should respond.

Let's do a thought experiment. I want you to imagine that you are at a train station, awaiting the arrival of someone you really love. Imagine the whole scene: it's your local train station. The sights (ticket barriers? Coffee shop? Angry ticket guy in a high-vis vest?), the smells (so many smells) and most importantly, how you are feeling. Where can you feel what you can feel? Are your fingers tingling? Is your heart beating fast? Maybe your belly is flipping a little. They have been away for six months and you have been longing for this moment. There you are, holding flowers* then, suddenly, you see your least favourite human – maybe it's the school bully, maybe it's a guy who broke your heart, maybe it's the grumpy neighbour who is always telling you to keep it down. How do you feel now? You catch each other's eyes. You refuse to drop the eye contact. In the end, your least favourite human breaks and walks off, refusing to look back. You feel like you won that exchange. And then, at the barriers, there they are – your love! Maybe you would run toward them, perhaps you would have your arms open, waiting. You might cry because you are so happy to see them. You go home together, hand in hand. It is super cute.

---

* Or something you know this person would like. If you are meeting me at a train station, I will want a Chelsea bun from Greggs.

From this simple imaginary exercise, you can see how varied and quickly your physical experience morphs from one stimulus to the next. You get a sense of what gestures or facial expressions you might have made. I felt warmth in my belly and butterflies as I waited for my love, but then tightness in my neck and shoulders when I saw my enemy. I felt a smirk cross my face as I won the eye contact battle and then, when I saw my love, I imagined myself holding them close to my chest, my heart soaring.

From our emotional response to any moment, movement and gesture will occur. Or as Viola Spolin puts it: 'For it is the physical manifestation of emotion, whether it is a quiet widening of the eyes or a violent throwing of a cup, that we can see and communicate.'

This is great for improv, but why might it be useful in life? For two reasons. One is that we rush through moments where we could sit in those emotions for longer. We choose words over the pregnant silence. If we can be more attuned to how we feel, if we can sit in those feelings, we will find it easier to embrace beautiful, meaningful moments and to tackle more difficult moments. In the UK, it sometimes seems that emotions are to be controlled rather than felt. How about you see that person you love, and you stand there in that love before you speak? How about you let that emotion inform what you want to say? When your child hugs you goodnight, how about you hug them a little bit longer and let them feel what you are feeling*, as well as saying, 'I love you'.

----

* Unless what you are feeling is: 'I can't believe you broke the downstairs window again!'

The second reason this body work is important to life is that, so often, we are making offers that we aren't aware of. The person(s) we are interacting with is picking up on them (consciously or subconsciously) and that is when conversation and intention can be misconstrued. You tell a friend that you'd love to go for dinner, but you keep wringing your hands, so they wonder if you are just being polite. You say you can't finish the filing this afternoon because you have an important meeting, but your colleague notices you can't look them in the eye. Something is not right, and if we are more aware of what our bodies are giving away, we can be more authentic in our interactions.

The Secret Gift of Listening to Your Body and Its Offers (Even the Painful Ones)

There are lots of reasons as to why we ignore our body's offers and responses, but the main one is often that they are uncomfortable. Let me tell you a story.

In 2017 I was hugely stressed. My anxiety was high. I was working too hard on a project that was not feeding my soul, with a whole lot of conflict within the group I was working in. I could feel the anxiety in my chest, but I would not acknowledge it. I knew, deep down, that I had to leave this project, but I couldn't. Rather, I felt like I couldn't. So, my anxiety was the result of a fight between my need to leave and my determination to stay, all of which I was refusing to investigate. I was just pushing through having a chest that was constantly tight, bursting into tears at inconvenient moments* and hosting a whole succession of mild panic attacks that made me appear to be losing my mind. Because I was a bit.

Typing this, I am well aware how ridiculous it sounds. Yes, these were all my body's physical offers, the very offers recommended by Viola Spolin and endorsed by me, the author of this incredibly useful book. My entire body was telling me, 'STOP THIS JOB,' but I refused to hear it. I had a confused sense of loyalty, and I had not yet worked out that it is a perfectly valid option to rescind loyalty if it is causing you huge amounts of personal damage.

The great thing about bodies is they don't give up making you offers. So there I was, weeping over my Gmail account for the umpteenth time, thinking I just needed to buck up[†], when I started getting incredible pains in my butt[‡]. Like a searing, shocking pain, as if I had shoved glass up my backside. One day, I went to the toilet, and there was blood. I was freaking out. I am so stressed and now my butt is bleeding? What is this? Obviously I thought the worst, so went straight to my doctor[§] who looked really disappointed that he was going to have to look at my butthole. I normally only go in for the contraceptive pill, so he was hoping for a nice easy bit of

----

* Is it ever actually convenient to burst into tears?

† The great English attitude to trauma: stop moaning and sort it out.

‡ Warning – this is about to get graphic. My mother was a butt physio, so I have minimal shame around sharing these things.

§ Praise be to the NHS.

prescription writing. Not today, doc. Get that torch up my butt.

It turned out, dear reader, that I had a tear in my butt called a fissure. You didn't think you were going to learn medical butt terminology from this book, did you? You're welcome. Anyone reading this book who has had a fissure is currently shivering with the memory of the immense pain that can be caused by these bad boys. They are about 2mm in length – tiny – but because they are in your butt, where there are loads of nerve endings, they hurt like hell. The doctor noted that stress was usually a major cause of fissures and asked if there was anything I could do to relax. Any changes I could make in my life. I knew exactly what I had to do.

I handed in my resignation and within days my butt was pain free. My body wanted me to stop doing work that harmed me, and the only way it could get me to listen was to make my butt bleed*. Pretty extreme and not very pretty. We ignore the offers our body gives us because sometimes the actual situation is more painful to process than the physical pain ... which gives you an idea of exactly how unhappy I was. But also how frighteningly willing I was not to admit to that. This is the cost of not listening to your own body's offers, people. It will literally be a pain in your butt.

---

* I went on a conflict resolution course once and told this story. The leader of the group replied: 'Let me tell you a story about my balls!' Turns out, I am not the only one who has had to be rescued by their crotch area.

If in Doubt, Move Your Body

Sometimes, your body is sending you clear messages you choose to ignore. Sometimes, you need to move your body to get the message. In *Showstopper!*, if we were stuck in a scene mentally, we realised we should move physically. Often, if we walked across the stage or sat down in a chair when feeling stuck verbally, we would discover what to say. It would just pop right into our heads, as if a gift from the heavens. This is not only way easier for the performer, but far more interesting for the audience. No longer were they watching two actors talking at each other – suddenly the movement connected with the dialogue. This should come as no surprise, I suppose. Motion and emotion are interconnected, as explored by prac-titioners of dance therapy, which encourages participants to use movement in the expression of the subconscious. Through dance, the physical movement connects the body to the mind and seems to have the effect of dislodging emotions that the client has been unable to release, so that these feelings might arrive into their conscience meaning that they can then begin to explore them more deeply*.

This speaks to me as an improviser because improvised shows only truly falter when we freeze in tension with the fear of getting it wrong or not knowing what to say. This marries with dance therapy theory, such as that of Trudi Shoop, world-renowned dance therapist. Shoop found that

---

* Maybe that is what they were trying to do with the 'Ancient Mariner'.

dance would draw mental health patients out of isolation, becoming responsive, rather than fearful, of human contact. If we hold ourselves rigid and do not allow ourselves to move physically, how can we expect our minds to be free to explore the vast expanse of our imaginations?

I started to explore this in my Improv Your Life workshops by asking people to move around the space, as if they were not having a good day. To remember how they hold themselves physically when they are not feeling great, and when they are masking how they are feeling with a version of themselves that they are frustrated with. The majority of the room interpreted this by looking to the floor, dragging their feet, hiding in corners, holding their shoulders up to their ears (I asked them to perform this tension as a role, ramping it up to 'one million percent' so as to play with the idea, rather than relive trauma). I then told the group that I would clap my hands and they could return to normal. The change of energy in the room on the clap was incredible! Here were these people, just ten seconds ago in the depths of despair and now, with a clap of the hand and a switch of their physicality, the class are holding themselves with a more open physicality, shoulders back, heads up, smiles creeping over their faces – a lightness returned to the entire room. It felt like we had discovered an actual life hack.

I took this back to *Showstopper!* rehearsals and asked everyone to act as they would, in the wings, if they were not feeling confident about the show. To exaggerate the tension and physical rigidity that comes with fear (we will call this Tension State 1 [TS1]). I then asked everyone to take on the physicality that comes when they are feeling fabulous in the show – they feel good as a performer, the show is going brilliantly (we will call this Tension State 2 [TS2]). The performers needed to remember how it feels to be in both these states, as we were going to flip between the two, on a clap. The *Showstopper!* team then improvised a huge song and dance number, starting in TS1 and, when I clapped my hands, switching to TS2. We went back and forth between the two states of tension and the results were phenomenal.

The awkward, painful-to-watch show in TS1 with uncomfortable, self-conscious actors suddenly became a beautiful, symbiotic performance in TS2. The ease with which this change could be made, simply by changing how the performers held their bodies, was a revelation. The performers felt that they had been given a secret recipe – yet it was so simple. When we notice tension we can drop it. If we can notice when our bodies are physically holding us back and we can find ways to release that, this simple act can completely change the experience of any situation.

Try this as an experiment next time you are having a chat. If you find you don't know what to say, release and move your body. It can be as simple as rolling your shoulders or uncrossing your legs. If your child is asking you for something you cannot supply and you feel stuck, move across the room. If you are in a conversation that is frustrating you, check for physical tension, release and breathe. If you are trying to finish a document and you just can't find the words, go for a walk. The more freedom we have in our physical selves, the less complicated our ability to communicate becomes. As

Ferris Jabr states in his article, 'Why Walking Helps Us Think', in *The New Yorker*: 'Because we don't have to devote much conscious effort to the act of walking, our attention is free to wander – to overlay the world before us with a parade of images from the mind's theatre. This is precisely the kind of mental state that studies have linked to innovative ideas and strokes of insight.'

Walking vast vistas can be useful for processing big thoughts, percolating ideas and working out what we think, as can crossing the room, looking out of the window or going to the kitchen to make a cup of tea. It is why TV detectives often have their revelation whilst doing something else: Inspector Morse prunes his roses and suddenly must call Lewis. Jessica Fletcher is changing her neck scarf and suddenly has to run back to the crime scene she has no real business being at. It's why speeches are given whilst being stood still ('I have collected my thoughts'), and the reason behind people working things out by pacing the room ('I am consolidating my thoughts'). Stillness represents certainty; movement represents rumination. If you aren't sure what to do about your difficult neighbour, take a walk. If you are having a frustrating conversation with your mum, cross to the other side of the room*. If in doubt, move.

---

* Sometimes leave the room and come back in a year.

Your Mind Is Your Body Is Your Mind

It's important that we look at what our bodies are telling us – what kinds of feelings are emerging from us in response to offers (verbal or non-verbal) received. Extreme offers are easier to navigate – someone is giving you threatening vibes, you get the hell out of there. The harder offers to decipher are the ones where the verbal and non-verbal do not align. The job offer that sounds great, but your stomach is turning. A favour requested by a good friend that is perfectly reasonable, but you feel uncomfortable for some reason. In these moments, we might need to sit with our feelings for a little longer. We might not be able to answer a request immediately. We may need time to think about our response. Taking time is good – it means we can be sure that the offers we make are genuine rather than hasty but well-meaning.

Our bodies make offers to us all the time. Check in with your body regularly and see if you can foster a sense of connection, a unity, between your mind and body. Your body might be trying to tell you something. Let your actions match your feelings.

Exercise Corner

SOLO

Go people-watching. Sit yourself in a café, a library or anywhere that you'll find people walking by, sitting chatting or meeting up. Observe how their bodies move. What silent offers are they making? Invent stories that go with their gestures. How would you act in the same situation? If it is possible without getting yourself in hot water, mirror their behaviour – see how it feels on your body. Explore how other people communicate with their bodies. Sometimes, when we put on other people's clothes, it is easier for us to recognise our own.

IN A PAIR

Move Then Talk

You and your friend are going to have a conversation, but you aren't allowed to speak until you have moved. This exercise is very artificial, but shows how much we don't notice what our bodies are saying before we respond verbally. Name your-selves A and B. Decide what you want to talk about – it could be your day, an event coming up – anything that is real to you both. Once you have decided, A will move across the room and then say the first thing that they want to. B then, after hearing what A has to say, allows the words to touch her and moves where feels right. There is no wrong, there is only what feels right. **B** similarly allows the words to touch them and moves in response to their impact. You might take a big stride, it might be a single step, it might be a hand on the hip. Keep this going until your conversation comes to an end. Remember, you cannot speak and move at the same time.

What did you notice about how the moving affected you? Did it feel different to how you speak in a normal conversation?

STATUS GAMES

I say status, you say ...? What do you say? Have you ever thought about status? I know I didn't until I started improvising. For some people, status is something they crave their entire life. For others, it is a thing that they update on Facebook. Our status, for most people, is not something we actively think about. So for the purposes of this chapter, I would like you to think of two types of status: professional status i.e. the status awarded to you by the role you play in society (consider the instantly high status you give a title like a doctor or a judge) and interpersonal status i.e. your social position relative to that of others. Your job or education might give you an assumed status, but it is the people around you that give you your immediate status and your behaviour that informs it. So, two doctors have the same societal status, but between the two of them, one might give the other higher status because they are in awe of them and their work, for example. Or one might see the other as lower status because they have a gravy stain down their white coat. We can have a low status judge (their wig slips, they are drunk, they fall off their chair) or a high status homeless person (they are wise, they outwit a thug, they are content).

Knowing where your status lies in any given situation can make all the difference in any kind of negotiation or exchange.

Once we have an awareness of status interplay, we can choose how we wish to play the game. Will we accept the status given? Will we have a status-off with the person we are meeting? Do we want to raise or lower the status of the person we are interacting with? If we have a particular outcome we wish to achieve, knowing our status will help us achieve it. Imagine the parent who goes to speak to the teacher without respecting their status in the classroom. That conversation is not going to go well – the parent needs to acknowledge that they are entering the teacher's space, and lower their status enough that the teacher knows the parent is respecting it. The teacher, equally, needs to respect the parent's wish to protect their child, whilst owning their status as educator. It can be tricky stuff to master but it's enlightening once you have unlocked the game.

Status is discovered through relationships between people, objects and space. Yes, even a room can affect your status.

Imagine yourself experiencing any of these encounters:

- Your headteacher's office at school when you were a kid.
- An awards ceremony in which you have a nomination.
- A shopping trip.

Give yourself a moment to think about how you might feel in each of those imagined situations. Really imagine them, and stay in that imagined space for a while. What happens? Who comes in? Most importantly, how is your status? Does your status stay the same or does it change?

Let's take the first situation, the headteacher's office. Here is one way that it could go. The office itself gives you a sense of foreboding. You might be in trouble, the headteacher might tell you off. In this case, your status is lowered – the room is not yours and holds the potential for discipline. The suggestion of the headteacher makes you feel a little helpless, knowing they have the authority in this situation. When the headteacher enters, they do not look at you. They sit at their desk and seem to write something in a big book marked 'Naughty Children'. Your status is lowered even further by their ignoring you. Eventually the headteacher looks at you and says, 'Detention'. They thrust the detention slip into your hand and point you to the door. They ignore your protests. You leave, despondent. Whilst your status has been continually lowered, the headteacher's status has stayed at a pretty constant high throughout.

This is only one way that the story might play out, because the status level can change the whole experience. If you feel very comfortable in the headteacher's office (perhaps you have been there numerous times) you might wander in and sit down without asking. You might casually ask the headteacher, 'What's up, teach?' If the headteacher likes your cheeky ways, they might gently remind you to call them by their full name, keeping your statues close, but still showing that they are a higher status than you. Although they have the official higher status, they are keeping their personal status lower than they might with another naughty student they like less. If the headteacher is fed up with your cheeky ways, they might shout at you, or do a terrifying 'teacher stare*' that makes you shrink off the chair, stand up and apologise, even though you aren't quite sure why. All of this is status play. Tiny shifts between folks that mean our status is constantly changing.

Let us now turn to the award ceremony example, which could be the complete opposite. It may make you feel elevated. Perhaps being a nominee gives you a feeling of higher status to the rest of the room. You sit and wait for the award to be announced – people congratulating you on your nomination – which raises your status even more. The people sat around you constantly raise your status with compliments. You are maintaining that status by accepting the compliments without deflecting them†. The awards are announced and ... you don't win. Suddenly, you feel your status trickle away. A woman on the table next door has won instead of you. Everyone on your table is now clamouring to congratulate her. Your status is lowered and you have to do the 'I am so happy for you' face. People give you 'never mind' smiles. Status is not fixed – it can shift in an instant. Whether

---

* Do you remember these? When your teacher could make you feel two inches tall, just by not blinking for a whole minute while they bore their eyes into you. This is many people's first experience with a status game. See also: mums when you chat back to them. Terrifying.

† You know when someone says: 'You look nice.' and you reply: 'No, I don't!' or 'I'm not sleeping at the moment!' – that is a status deflection. By accepting the compliment, your status is raised ever so slightly. It can be uncomfortable, so instead of just saying, 'Thank you,' we say, 'Look at this spot on my chin!' Which they hadn't noticed before, but now they can't un-see it.

that be an external shift (losing the award) or an internal shift (you change the way you respond to the people around you).

Finally, the shopping trip. You go to the supermarket. You most likely feel neutral or seemingly without status when you think about this example. It's just a place to buy your groceries. However, it is in the supermarket that we learn even inanimate objects can raise or lower our status. The self-checkout refuses to scan your yoghurt. You try four times, and then have to type in the crazy long barcode number. You keep getting it wrong. A queue is building up behind you. As you get more frustrated, your hands start to shake and there is no one to assist you. The self-checkout asks if you want to cancel your shopping. You scream at the machine, 'No I don't, you arse-wipe!' You signal to the assistant that you need some help, actually. They come over, and in one manoeuvre manage to scan your yoghurt and make you look like a numpty. Now the assistant is also high status. You can feel the judgement from the queue* and somehow, you have gone from a relaxed, neutral human to a low status, gibbering wreck. 'Thank you for shopping at Tesco' seems to have a sarcastic tone to it. You leave and vow only to be served by humans from now on.

---

* I'd like to be reassuring and say, 'It's all in your head,' but who am I kidding? Queues make people judgy.

Status Transactions

All of these moments are known as 'status transactions'. Each person in the interaction is responsible for the giving and taking of status. It is not only in your eyes that your status has changed, but in the eyes of the people around you. It doesn't necessarily matter what you want your status to be – it is given and taken. We cannot demand status, although we can try.

Let me tell you a story.

In my last year of school, I was made head girl*. I was very proud of this and felt quite special. My status, in my eyes, was raised above the other students. I walked around the school grounds with my head held high, hoping the other students would notice me and perhaps ask for life advice. Suddenly, a year seven pupil approached me and said, 'Excuse me! Are you the head girl?' My chest swelled with pride. What might this 11-year-old cherub need from me – the wise woman of the school? Exam advice? Was she being bullied and needed my calm, nurturing 17-year-old ways to bring her and the assailant together?

'There's a dead pigeon over there.' She said, pointing at a rotting bird corpse. 'Probably needs moving.' Then she walked off. I thought being head girl meant I was of a new, higher

---

* Whenever people find out that I was head girl of my school, they are never surprised. I am still not sure whether to take this as an insult or not.

status and this munchkin destroyed that with one request to remove a dead pigeon. I was not a revered member of society. I was, in fact, to this student, just someone to do rubbish jobs she didn't want to. I took the pigeon to reception where they said: 'What am I going to do with a dead pigeon?' To which I didn't really have an answer. Turns out, no one has 'deal with dead pigeons' on their job description. It's probably why there are so many in Trafalgar Square.

Status in Comedy

All comedy is based in status transactions. The above story is only funny because my perceived status is removed, like a rug being pulled from beneath me. Status play is at the heart of stand-up comedy. The stand-up comedian arrives on stage and immediately lowers their status, your status or the status of another group:

'Good evening! My name is Pippa Evans and I am aware I look like a young John Lithgow.'

(Lowering my status by saying I look like an 80-year-old man).

'Good evening, Chelsea! I am a needy performer. Ladies, if you've had a lot of Botox, could you just hold up a sign that says: "enjoying the show".'

(Lowering the status of a group in an affluent area or 'punching up').

'Good evening, Durham! I'm so glad to be here. I was in Newcastle last night, so I am glad to be anywhere!'

(Routine line used to ally with the area you are playing by slagging off the next town they have historical beef with).

A fantastic comic is able to play with status constantly through a show. Go to any stand-up show and you will be able to see this being done brilliantly. They will manipulate the status between themselves and the audience (Me and You) and those in the comedy club and those outside the comedy club (Us and Them). When a comic is floundering, it isn't necessarily that their material is no good, it is more likely they haven't got their status transactions in order. The audience feels too far above the comic, or too judged.

The Canadian-born, British stand-up Katherine Ryan is excellent at this. She is able to flick between mocking herself, mocking the audience and mocking the world, and we still love her. She balances who her 'victims' are with such precision, that she can be biting and provocative whilst still being charming. We are in her gang, under her spell and only the foolhardy would heckle her (another status game) because she would slam them right back down to the status position they deserve. Audience is always slightly below comic, but they should never know that.

Status in Improv

Keith Johnstone talks extensively about status in his book, *Impro*. He started teaching it because he noticed a lack of naturalism in improvised conversations. 'Try to get your status just a little above or below your partner's I said, and I insisted that the gap should be minimal. The actors seemed to know exactly what I meant and the work was transformed. The scenes became "authentic", and actors seemed marvellously observant. Suddenly we understood that every inflection and movement implies a status, and that no action is due to chance, or really "motiveless".'

To allow a class to experience status first-hand, I ask them to imagine that status is on a scale of one to ten, where one is the lowest and ten is the highest. I then pass out pieces of paper with these numbers written on them, playing only with ten players, and no one seeing which status anyone else has. The ten players then move around the room, playing out their status silently. They can manifest it however they wish – they might use their faces, their walk, their energy to express this status but there can be no talking. After a few minutes of moving and observing, the ten players are asked to arrange themselves in order of status, from one to ten, without conferring. Ninety-nine per cent of the time, the group get it spot on.

I ask the class how they knew what status each other was. They reply:

'Kate was dragging her feet, so she seemed low status.'

'Gary had his nose in the air and wouldn't make eye contact, so he was high!'

'Corina seemed pretty content, so I guessed she was somewhere in the middle.'

All of these are correct observations and there will be thousands more. Tiny offers that are being given off by the players to show where they believe they hold their status.

This is excellent practise for people to explore this topic. Once you play with status, you start to recognise the status you tend to navigate in the world. Have a little think of how you interact with someone you might consider high status – a doctor, a police officer, a parent. How does your behaviour change compared to how you are perhaps with your good friends, where your statuses are probably the same?

It's important to notice our own response to perceived status because sometimes we are so impressed by someone's title that we give them a huge amount of freedom in their behaviour – in turn lowering ourselves so much that we forget that we can respect someone's social status and still allow ourselves the status we deserve. For example, I was in hospital for a routine operation and a new doctor I hadn't seen before came to my bedside. He explained that actually I didn't need the operation so I should go home. I started to say, 'OK, you know best,' because who am I to question a doctor? I am a comedian in a gown with my butt hanging out*. I realised that I was giving him so much status, I wasn't going to question this quite sudden and perhaps incorrect choice. I was still ill in a hospital bed, after all.

So I covered my butt (raise status ever so slightly) and said, 'The other three doctors seemed to think it was necessary, can you check my bloods again just to be sure?' He didn't like being questioned (lowered his status a little bit) but to be fair, he did as I asked. He returned ten minutes later and said, 'Ah yes, actually, having checked your bloods, you do need the

---

* There's my butt again.

operation. Sorry about that.' So checking my status interaction, in this instance, may have saved my life.

Equal Status Among Friends

A friend of mine recently commented that he doesn't invite his mum to his social events because his friends behave so differently when she is there. His mum has official social status (an elder) and is greatly respected by the group. This makes perfect sense, from an improv point of view. If you have a group of characters and one is hugely different in status to the rest of them, it will be impossible for us to hear what the characters really think of the high status person. The high status individual will need to leave the space. A boss needs to leave the staffroom for the workers to talk about how they really feel about them. A police officer can reprimand a group of people and they will most likely be compliant, until she walks away and hears the mutters of: 'What a jobsworth'. And so, my friend's mum, as delightful as she is, can alter the atmosphere of a party because his friends hold her in such high regard. Imagine the Queen popping by for dinner – it's going to make you behave differently, no matter your opinion on the monarchy.

Friends tend to be on the same level when it comes to status transactions. You will make micro adjustments in conversation, but generally you hold each other in equal regard. If you have a friend who is always playing low status in your group or whom you find yourself significantly lower in status to, it will be a tricky friendship. Also true if you have one super high status pal. There needs to be a sense of equilibrium or we are back to not being able to say what we want to say until the high status person leaves the space. It's the story of every teen movie ever made – the geek who got pretty gets to hang out with the cool girls, only to realise she can't be herself with them, so she goes back to the geeks. It's all status – geek girl thinks she wants to raise her status to being in the cool gang, but then realises that to maintain that status it comes at a cost to herself, so she returns to a lower, but equal, status (usually transforming the 'cool' girls status as she goes).

Playing With Status

Improv is a great place to play with the idea of status, not just so we can explore how different status positions affect us, but also because it will inevitably be funny. In a class, I will ask two students to play together. One will begin as high status and the other low status. I will ask them to be as playful in their status work as they possibly can be, and by the end of the scene, to have switched status. If I give them a scenario, such as a shoe shop, where we have a customer/assistant relationship, we already have assumptions about who is higher and who is lower.

Let us start with the customer at a higher status and watch the switch:

Customer: (Not looking at the assistant) Excuse me. I'd like to try these in an 11. Now.

Shop Assistant: (Holding the shoe, then almost dropping it) Yes . . . ummm . . . just a minute . . .

Customer: (Interrupting) I don't have much time – I am flying to Geneva tonight.

Shop Assistant: (Attempting to make conversation) Oooh . . . I've never been on a plane.

Customer: (Delivered with flair) I own all the planes!

Shop Assistant: (Questioning) Do you . . . umm . . . need all the planes?

Customer: (Indignant) What do you mean?

Shop Assistant: (Getting the shoes) It just . . . seems greedy to have all the planes.

Customer: Well, I don't have *all* the planes. I mean, I, I, I own a few.

Shop Assistant: (Putting the shoe on the customer) How many is a few?

Customer: Three.

Shop Assistant: Three?

Customer: Alright, one. I own one plane.

Shop Assistant: (Looking at the shoe) Are you sure you are a size 11?

Customer: (Sheepishly) It might be more like a large eight.

Shop Assistant: (Sympathetic) Right. I'll see if I can find some 'large eights'.

Customer: (More sheepish) Maybe a huge five would be even better.

Shop Assistant stands up, looks at the customer and pats him
on the shoulder as he goes off to the storeroom. Customer
sits down on a chair, looking deflated.

Customer: (Shouting back) It's a big plane!

Shop Assistant: (Shouting from off stage) Is it?

Customer: (Quietly) No.

I love this scene. We see the status switch clearly, as the Customer is revealed to be bending the truth to achieve their preferred status and the Shop Assistant goes from cowering before this self-made man to realising they have nothing to feel intimidated by. We see that the Shop Assistant stops saying 'Ummm' and speaking in incomplete sentences. The Customer goes from being flamboyant and demanding to defeated, as he sits on a chair and waits for his not-so-big shoes.

Once we start to notice status transactions, we can use this information to help us navigate situations where something seems off with an interaction. It can bring clarity to what is happening in areas where the status transaction is not playing out so clearly. When you are in a job interview, perhaps, and the status seems to be constantly shifting: the interviewer appears dismissive but then is suddenly enthralled by your story about a previous job, raising your status with their new found attention. You are surprised by this shift and begin to stumble on your words. You feel their attention go – your status lowered again. It is confusing, in the moment, but less so when you have a status lens to see through. Parents in my classes often use the example of their teenagers shifting from sweet, obedient children to hormone-filled teens. Suddenly they seem to have the highest status imaginable and hold their parent in such disregard they can't even look at them. The status shift comes when the teen wants something and suddenly, they lower their status, compliment the parent and then ask for a Nintendo Switch. When the parent reasonably explains why it isn't possible (desperately trying not to play status games), the teen rages about the unfairness of life and tells the parent how dreadful they are: the extreme high status returns*. When we translate these interactions into status, they suddenly make a bit more sense, if not necessarily easier to navigate. At least the dynamics of what is happening don't seem so alien.

If you find yourself in a status game, it is up to you if you want to play or walk away. In his incredible book, *Games People Play*, Eric Berne suggests that in the playing of any social game (an argument with a friend, a conversation with a waiter, a confrontation with a colleague – take your pick) there are some variables to consider in:

1. **Tenacity**: Some people give up their games easily, others are persistent.
2. **Intensity**: Some people play their games in a relaxed way, others are more tense and aggressive . . .

These variables converge to make the games either gentle or violent.

---

* Parenting sounds like so much fun so much of the time!

You might be having a fun status transaction with a friend making jokes with each other. If this is done in a relaxed way, where status is flowing freely between the two of you, it will continue to be fun. If someone suddenly takes a joke to heart and feels hurt, they may start to play with more aggression. The status switches from low to high will become much wider and deeper, and what started as a fun game is now likely to turn into a row.

Kids do this all the time. I remember playing with a boy called Josh when I was about nine. There was a pear tree outside on the street and all the pears, brown and squishy, had fallen on the floor so we were throwing them at each other, for fun, because that is what kids do*. Whoever gets hit by a pear loses status, of course. We threw them back and forth, each of us taking turns to be the victor. Suddenly, Josh picked up a huge armful of pears and pelted me with them till I was weeping for him to stop. He did not want to the game to end with us equal status. He had to end up high. Wasn't childhood fun?

I don't want you to think that status transactions are always negative experiences – they just make for great examples. We notice these more because painful experiences stay with us longer. In fact, we use status to help each other, to raise each other in moments of need and to support our friends, family and colleagues. You raise your friend's status when you give them a compliment, when you support them through a break-up and remind them what an excellent

---

* We didn't need a Nintendo Switch in those days.

human they are. Your status is raised when someone opens a door for you or listens to what you have to say. Simply giving someone the time of day raises their status because it says: 'What you have to say is worth my attention.' On a great date, flirting is a constant status game, raising and lowering each other to show growing affection or sexual attraction. Your date tells you that you have wonderful eyes (raising your status) and you tell them they have wonderful taste (raising theirs and yours further). They tease you by noting you are pretty confident (slightly lowering your status) and you continue the game by telling them it's hard not to be when you are as excellent as you are (raising your status back). It's like a game of status ping-pong, creating the frisson than makes that first kiss so electric – because finally you arrive at the status agreement – you both think the other is pretty great. Your statuses match in that moment as your lips meet and the status ping-pong continues, all the way home.

Have a go at raising and lowering your status next time you are talking with a friend. To lower it, add uncertain pauses in your sentences, keep dropping eye contact or shuffle your feet. To raise it, lift your head up, drop your shoulders, hold eye contact or stand with your weight evenly distributed on both legs. Play around with other ways you move and speak, discovering what occurs in the status transaction. What is your friend doing that affects your status? The smallest move can make the biggest impact.

Status Conflicts in the Public Sphere

Status conflicts arise when people do not agree on the status they are being given or that is being requested, which can cause deadlock until one side agrees to relinquish or adapt their status position. These status disagreements are constantly being played out in the public sphere. The #MeToo movement, for example, is a rejection of the status given to women who have been the victims of sexual assault. Women have risen up and refused to remain silent about their ordeals and demanded to be listened to. They seek a status equal to that of men, where one group's pain is not silenced for the other's comfort. The Black Lives Matter movement continues to demand the raising of status for Black people. Most recently, the death of George Floyd in 2020 caused Black people and allies around the world to stage protests yet again, demanding equality and the dismantling of white supremacy. Black people refusing to be held at a lower status is proving hugely challenging to those who do not want their own status to change. Until men are held accountable for their sexual violence towards women, men will continue to hold a higher status in society's eyes. Until Black people are afforded equal status to white people, Black people will continue to suffer the hidden (and not so hidden) status transactions that play out in society. These movements will not rest until there is an agreement and a resetting of their status in society.

During Donald Trump's presidency, we endured a fascinating character when it comes to status play. He refused to be anything but high status. He was not interested in the flex-ibility of status because, in his mind, he is continually of a high status, no matter how often his incompetence as a leader is pointed out or his fake tan is mocked. He refused, in many respects, to play the status game. He is outside of the game, which is why we find him so fascinating. He is playing a differ-ent game to everyone else, on his own. Top Trumps, perhaps, where his is the only card available.

Thinking about Trump made me consider who I thought was his absolute opposite. The first person who came into my mind was the Dalai Lama. The Dalai Lama also holds a high status position as 'his holiness' but does not play status games to solidify his place in the world. As such, he is almost beyond status. Trump is only able to exist by his external status but the Dalai Lama has cultivated his internal status, whereby he knows his worth and needs no external rewards for his inner state of mind. It is no surprise that Trump, who has faced minimal challenges to his social status (billionaire businessman, former president of the USA) would have minimal relationship with his inner status, whereas the Dalai Lama who has lived a life of exile from his homeland of Tibet has had no choice but to reach for his inner status. The deeper we look into ourselves, the less need for external status confirmation is needed.

Status Abuse

Unfortunately, people take advantage of their status all the time. Harvey Weinstein is the perfect example of a status abuser. He abused his status as a movie producer by raising women's immediate status – luring them to his rooms with the promise of a job. Flattered that a movie producer had shown interest in their work, they would go to meet him, where he would make sexual demands of them. Following his initial sexual abuse, he would destroy or raise their external status (blacklisting actresses from his productions for non-compliance or rewarding them with parts in films), dependent on how compliant they were with his wishes.

This is why knowing status and playing status games in an improvised setting is great learning, especially for women and anyone vulnerable to abuse. If we understand what different status games feel like, in a non-threatening environment, we will be more likely to notice status imbalance when we are in an uncomfortable or even dangerous situation.

External Status

As a recovering achiever, I understand the need for external status raising. It took a while to link the status work I had done in improv to my obsessive need to do impressive things. It slowly dawned on me that there were very few jobs I did because I felt passionate about them or even wanted to do them. Instead, I took jobs because other people would be impressed by my accolades.

It is not an aversion to success, but rather an aversion to the need to succeed in other people's eyes to be of value to the world. I have worked with CEOs in companies who are doing the work that satisfies them and they are good at. Their status is a by-product of doing what they love. I have also worked with high-ranking officials who are miserable because they have achieved what they thought they wanted, but when they got there, it didn't provide them with anything like the life satisfaction they thought it would. So, are you getting your life satisfaction from the status you have gained or the life you lead?

Social status is a part of life. How we are treated and how we treat others can often be reduced down to status transactions. Next time you have a conversation, notice who is raising your status and who is lowering it (it could be you!). Notice which status you tend to default to and see if that is a status you are happy in. Most importantly, check in with that external status. Let's all be less Trump, more Dalai Lama.

Exercise Corner

SOLO

Write down any examples of times when you felt your status was lowered. It could be a meeting, a date, an encounter in the street. What did they do? What did they say? Were you signalling being low status somehow?

Do the same for when you felt your status being raised. What could you have done differently? Would you like to have done anything differently or were you happy with the status transaction?

IN A PAIR

Raise My Status

Have a conversation and see if, with each line, you can raise each other's status. For example:

Person A: You look amazing today!

Person B: Thank you, I used that shampoo you gave me for my birthday.

Person A: I never thanked you for my amazing birthday present. It was so generous.

Person B: You don't need to thank me – you are the best friend a gal could have.

Person A: I think you must be talking to a mirror because you are the best friend a gal could have.

Person B: No, you are!

Person A: No, you are!

It can go on forever. Be as ridiculous as you like. Enjoy being flattered and more importantly, notice what it is to have your status constantly raised.

The Eagle of Despair

Sometimes I feel despair in my head like an eagle. It's talons clawing into my mind. And because it speaks with a grave, intelligent voice, I find it hard to ignore. 'You are crap, you are. You're crap.' And I have to agree, because it sounds like he reads Shakespeare and other old things. And he says:

'You'll never be good enough to be on a panel show.'

And I say, 'But I don't want to be on a panel show.'

And he says, 'Yes. Yes you do. All you want is to be on a panel show.'

And then I turn on *Woman's Hour* and they tell me I am letting down all women by not wanting to be on a panel show.

And then the Eagle of Despair picks me up by my skull and flies me to a TV studio where Jimmy Carr starts barking at me. They say that's his laugh, but I am pretty sure he is just guarding his territory.

And I make jokes about Melinda Messenger's boobs and they say, 'Be more current,' so I make jokes about Jodie Marsh's boobs and they say, 'Be more current,' so I make jokes about FGM and they say, 'Too far. She went too far'. And then they edit the show so that it seems that I am just laughing at Jon Richardson and flicking my hair occasionally. And then the Eagle of Despair says, 'It's your own fault. You shouldn't have worn that top.' And I say, 'You told me to wear this top,' and he says, 'What do I know about fashion? I'm an eagle!'

I tell myself that I spend too much time with the Eagle of Despair. I should spend more time with the Raven of Self Confidence but he's always outside, shagging squirrels.

Perhaps you have a similar 'friend' who likes to visit. Do not give them an access all areas pass. The Eagle thinks it's there to help you, but if we give it too much attention, it takes over and stops us ever stepping into the unknown. Very helpful if you are a cave person or a forest dweller, being warned not to eat the mushrooms or pet the dragon. Not so helpful if you want to ask someone out or do a presentation on the latest sales figures.

The Eagle may perch there for a long time, but eventually, as we learn to stop listening to their panic and vitriol, their talons will loosen their grip. For many years, I performed improv shows with the Eagle gripping on tightly as I made whole rooms of people laugh. I would leave the stage and the Eagle would remind me of anything I did that didn't work, would focus on all the moments where there was a lull or a joke fell flat or my voice cracked, instead of the roaring laughter and the rounds of applause when a scene finished. Slowly, over time, I managed to untangle the Eagle's words from the reality of the situation. To notice that while, yes, that joke hadn't worked, there were some fantastic moments that needed to be noticed too. And slowly the Eagle's grip was loosened.

Now, when the Eagle is loud, I realise that I must be tired, or my anxiety is rising. The Eagle's presence is a warning system for my needing to take care of myself. And that is the only time I listen to the Eagle. Because he is just trying to take care of me. But he is also an eagle. He can't put me to bed, and if he made me dinner, it would be a load of carrion, dumped on the kitchen floor. So I thank the Eagle for his warning, check in to see whether there is anything that needs my attention, and then get on with my day.

If you have a particular negative voice that likes to point out every little error, I highly recommend giving it a name. It becomes much easier to separate those thoughts once they have been given an identity – like Derek* or MangoChops. A name that seems silly to you so that you aren't intimidated by them.

Start to notice when Derek appears. Is it always just before something where there is a risk of failure? Is it when there is the possibility of rejection? Once you know when Derek appears, you will be able to understand what Derek is trying to save you from. So you can thank Derek, and then decide if Derek is right to be concerned or if he is just being over-protective. Once we get past Derek, we can get past the fear of failing. Because failure is the only way to learn.

-----

* Apologies if you are called Derek. I find the name Derek inherently funny and can never find someone called Derek intimidating. Even if they were holding a gun to my head, I think I'd have to stifle a giggle.

CURIOSITY DIDN'T KILL THE CAT: IT WOKE HER UP

Showstopper! was doing an eight-week run in Toronto, Canada. We were so excited. Eight-week runs for improv shows in theatres are gold dust. In preparation, we went to town on the research. Performing improv in a different country means not just being aware of their local and national customs but having an active curiosity for it. What might a Canadian audience want a musical about? Let's make sure we have laid the groundwork. Whilst improvisation is made up on the spot, it is done so using the knowledge and experiences of the improvisers, which means we need to keep expanding our knowledge and experiences.

We realised quite quickly that there are some things audiences are happy for us to not know and make up completely (usually obscure historical references or pop culture) and other things they will be disappointed by if we haven't made the effort to research them (big events, significant dates and Celine Dion*). We studied all the Canadian musicals (there are more than you think – *My Fur Lady*, anyone?), Canadian history

---

* Never insult Celine Dion in Toronto. I learned this the hard way.

and culture (First Nations people, the geography, the language divide between the English and French speakers) and local Toronto titbits (the CN Tower, Toronto Maple Leafs [ice hockey team], BeaverTails [a pastry/heart attack in a napkin]). We arrived for our run wearing imaginary mortarboards, having graduated from Canadian Curiosity School.

The night of the first show arrived. *Showstopper!* begins with a host character asking the audience where they want the musical to take place, while the rest of the cast wait in the wings, listening out for our fate.

'Where would you like it set?' the host asked the crowd. We stood backstage, imagining what the audience might say. A freezing night in Winnipeg, perhaps? The meeting where they decided to use a maple leaf on the flag? The Winter Olympics of 1988?

'A 7-Eleven!' came a voice from the audience. The rest of the crowd roared with laughter, applauding and stamping their feet and so it was decided. We would improvise a musical set in a Canadian 7-Eleven called 'Brain Freeze'.

It just so happens, I am a specialist in 7-Elevens. I have loved them ever since we had them in the UK in the 90s (they were consequently sold to Budgens in 1998). One of their most famous products is a drink called the Slurpee®* and I love them. Any time I am in America or anywhere a 7-Eleven might

---

* The Slurpee® is like a superior Slush Puppy. A frozen blended drink of huge sugar content and bright colours. It is the drink *The Simpson's* have as a Squishy in the Kwik-E-Mart. It can put you in a diabetic coma from 200 yards.

appear (Hong Kong, Australia or Norway, for example), I have to go inside. I take in all the colours and smells and sounds. I look at all the candy and the crisps and I wonder who would buy that very sad-looking hot dog in their warm food counter. It's a mix of nostalgia and amazement at how good we are at creating junk food. And I always, always, always have to buy a Slurpee®.

When we arrived in Toronto, the first thing I did was find the nearest 7-Eleven and pick up one of those tasty frozen drinks. I saw all the new flavours and noticed an advertising campaign with the slogan 'Brain Freeze' being used to promote Slurpees® that summer. And so it came to pass that it was not our studious work in researching Canada that would get us off to a flying start in Toronto, but my weird fascination about a chain of convenience stores. My point? Get curious beyond your remit. You never know what kind of knowledge is going to help you one day.

Improvisers Need to Be Curious

To be a great improviser, we need to be curious about the worlds we create, the world we live in and how we exist in those worlds. We need to be curious about big things and small things in our real and imaginary world so we might know them better and be able to draw on different experiences, perspectives and knowledge of that which is all around us.

In the real world it is so easy to be on automatic pilot. To lose our curiosity. To fall back on 'This is the way we've always done it', rather than ask questions that may lead to a different way. Being stuck in our ways rather than experiencing and absorbing the ways and wisdom of other worlds. For we are all living in different worlds in the smallest of ways and that demands a degree of fascination from us. Monica Gaga, the excellent improviser and facilitator, has an exercise about lunch boxes. She puts the students into pairs and gets them to talk about what they had in their lunch boxes at school. Once they have discussed it, they share it with the group and it is amazing how different those lunch boxes can be. In a particular workshop I attended, we had everything from sandwiches to tiffin tins, stuffed palm leaves to sloppy school dinners. This exercise touched me because it was such a simple way of showing the diversity of experience. The many worlds we have all lived in, when we might have assumed that because we are in the same room, we have the same experiences. Being curious of other people's experiences can only be expansive for us; enriching the worlds we go on to create together and enabling empathy to develop as we learn how others live in the world.

Curiosity when we are in an improv show will create huge amounts of texture. What do I mean by texture? The bits of the show that allow the audience to experience it in 4-D. By adding details from our huge communal bank of experience, we fill the stage with more of the world for the audience to see in their imaginations. The more detail we give, the more the audience is able to see what we see (although they will, in one sense, see what we see how *they* see it).

For example, if I say to you, 'There is a house', it is a very basic offer, leaving a lot of room for interpretation. Maybe your imagined house is a terraced one, like in *Coronation Street*, or perhaps it is a spooky house on a hill or maybe it is a standard fairy tale two-up, two-down with a nice front door and a little path. There is no way for me to know that the house in my head looks like the one in yours. To make sure we are experiencing the same house, we need to add the detail, which we can find through richer description. Like this:

There is a house in a field, with broken windows. The roof has tiles missing and is a dull, grey colour. An old guy sits on a tractor and ploughs the golden corn field around it. He won't go within ten feet of the building, though. The corn there has grown right up to the top windows.

Suddenly, we can even *feel* the house. By embellishing the house's description through curiosity, using, 'If this is true then what else is true?' we are expanding the picture, adding colour and detail such that it draws an emotional response from the audience. How did you feel about the original house I offered you? How do you feel about this house? Which one are you more curious about? I would hazard a guess that it is the latter. The audience's curiosity is provoked when the improviser plays with their own curiosity.

Why Might We Stop Being Curious?

We are all born curious. Children are so curious that parents spend the first five years of their child's life in and out of A&E.

'What happened to Saj's arm?'

'Oh he wanted to see if he was a squirrel, so he jumped off a tree.'

Kids explore without the fear of consequence.

I remember deciding to lay my mum's full length mirror from my bed to my brother's bed, to see if I could make a bridge. I lifted it up with great effort and placed it between the two mattresses. I walked across it, gently and was amazed that it worked. Excitedly, I opened the window and screamed out to my brother, who was playing in the garden 'Charlie! Come and try the bridge I built!'

While Charlie came upstairs, I had another thought.

'If I can walk across the bridge, I wonder if I can jump?'

I can literally see this moment in my head in slow motion as I bounced on the bed and then landed in the middle of the mirror-bridge. It smashed in half, bits of glass flying everywhere and a massive chunk going into my foot. Charlie arrived in the room to find me surrounded by broken mirror, blood pouring out of my foot crying: 'The bridge broke'. I learned a lot about bridges and weight distribution that day. Also, that full length mirrors are very expensive. Sorry, Mum.

We must look to children to find the key back to our own curiosity and why it is important. Psychologist Dr Jamie Jirout, in an article for Parent Circle magazine, said this of curiosity: 'It is hard for children to be curious if they don't feel safe exploring and asking questions. At the same time, children must also face some uncertainty and learn to be comfortable with that uncertainty, while learning how to resolve it.'

Now read the above quote again but replace the word 'children' with 'adults'.

With the word 'adult' subbed in, it still rings true. If we could be a little more curious and a little more happy to ask questions, rather than believe we have all the answers, perhaps we might find uncertainty less terrifying. And yet, how safe is it for us to be curious as adults? How often have we felt ourselves to be in positions where we are encouraged to give false confidence rather than wise vulnerability? Children have people to clear up after them, to talk them through the one hundred WHYs they ask every day. Yet we, as adults, often have to do that for ourselves. We have to be the curious child and the sensible parent. If we are working a job (or two or three), running a household, looking after kids or aged parents, there is no wonder we find it hard to create time for curiosity. No, I don't want to be curious, I want a nap and a bowl of cheese Doritos. Forget curiosity, I just don't want to think.

Sometimes it is lack of time and exhaustion that stops us being curious. Sometimes it is that we want to think we have all the answers already. We are not willing to be seen as 'lesser' by still learning.

In their fantastic book and creativity manual, *The Universal Traveller*, Don Koberg and Jim Bagnall state: 'False pride stands in the way of creativity by inhibiting us from asking key questions, thus stifling the key requisite for curiosity.'

It can be a hard one to accept – pride as an obstacle to our own curiosity. As improvisers, we must never get complacent, as we are forever thrown into new situations with new show mates, new suggestions and new worlds that whilst we perform with the confidence of someone who knows exactly what to do, we have to explore with the naivety of someone who has only an inkling.

I used to be a real pretender. I would nod when someone mentioned something they expected me to know. I would laugh at jokes I didn't get and if questioned because my face had clearly betrayed me, I would bluff my way out. I did not like not knowing things. That was until I was hanging out with my friend Olivia one day. Olivia is perhaps the cleverest person I know in all senses. She is wise like an owl and has many degrees and accolades so she is also officially clever according to the government. She is life wise and book smart. You could ask her about Greek mythology and also if you should sleep with Gary from accounts.

One day we were talking about something and almost every second question she said, 'Sorry – what's that? I don't know what that means.' I couldn't believe it. 1) I knew something she didn't know and 2) she was cool about it. I said to her: 'Olivia, I'm so amazed that you just ask when you don't know something.' and she said, 'Well how will I ever know if I don't ask?' and that my friends, is why she is wise like an owl. If we don't ask, we'll never know. If we aren't curious, we will never expand any of our knowledge: of ourselves, each other or the world.

Curiosity Sounds Soft

Sometimes it is the word itself that stops us from engaging. 'Curiosity' feels like a frivolous idea. An activity from a Lewis Carroll book, suitable only for children following talking rabbits down holes and having play adventures. Yet curiosity is the act of an explorer. Not just of the jungle or the mountains but of life. You can be curious about facts, learning knowledge that will push you further in your career or dreamed future. Curious about languages and communication that will help you better express yourself. You can be curious about emotions, smells, tastes. Imagine the child in you saying, 'What's that? Why? How?' in every situation your curiosity is piqued. You can follow your curiosity for 30 seconds or 30 years*. Your curiosity can be fierce, arming you with knowledge to fight your battles. Your curiosity can be applied to justice, to social movements, to politics. Curiosity is not frivolous – it is vital.

Eve Started It

We need to ask questions to move forward. Imagine, if you will, a world without questions. Imagine a child never asks, 'Why?' ever again. No engineer asks, 'What does that do?' No

---

* Also fine to be somewhere in between this timescale. It is not a binary choice.

scientist ever says, 'What if?' In her essay, 'The Apple', Betsy de Lotbinière speaks of 'What if' in reference to the Garden of Eden: 'Eve was told "don't" and burned to answer the first ever "what if?" Risking that first bite makes this first woman the first artist, the first philosopher, the first revolutionary – the first scientist.'

I love this interpretation of the story. This was the first question, and it was *before* biting the apple. It was the offer of knowledge and a curiosity that led to change. 'What if' may be our most powerful curious question. It makes us all artists (creating creative solutions), philosophers (exploring ideas), revolutionaries (acting for change) and scientists (forming hypotheses to be tested). It makes us pioneers in the kitchen (I've run out of tomato sauce. What if I use ketchup instead?) and explorers in the staff room (Class 2B are out of control. What if I let them teach the class today?). If something spikes your curiosity, chuck a 'What if?' at it and see where your mind wanders.

Isn't Curiosity Just Following Your Obvious?

No, but they are bedfellows. Like Success and Failure, you cannot have curious without obvious. To follow your obvious is to listen to your intuition – curiosity is about expanding the circle of knowledge about yourself, each other and the world. Imagine it as all the knowledge you gain which enables you to follow your obvious. The berries you gather along the journey, from bushes that line the road. Following your obvious is a forward momentum, it is action. Curiosity is expansive sideways. Curiosity need have no reason to exist than to just be. You can learn about ships and not join the navy, you can study all the different cake recipes and never enter *The Great British Bake Off*. Curiosity does not have to link to ambition, although it can.

Imagine curiosity like an elasticated waistband that just keeps expanding out. An ever-widening circle. It can never be finished because there is so much to know. Don't be overwhelmed by that – be amazed. Curiosity needs courage. As our worlds expand, we must continue to question them. To ask more of them, to explore every nook and cranny. Be curious to find out things you don't know about; the things you think you know and even more about the things you don't.

Whether it's Googling, wandering, wondering or questioning: get curious.

Exercise Corner

SOLO

This will take at least 30 minutes, maybe more, so do this exercise when you have time to give it your full attention. Open a news app (or actual newspaper if you are retro cool) and choose a story that catches your interest. Read the article, and the moment something appears in it that you have a question about, get into a search engine wormhole. See how far your curiosity about this story can take you. Imagine the story as the centre of a spider diagram, from which you are going to draw lots of extra information that fills out the picture.

If it is a report about a climate issue, for example, perhaps they will mention, 'carbon footprint'. If you are like me, you might know about it vaguely, but not deeply. Get more curious about that footprint – find a definition that speaks to you, a video that explains it in a way that helps to understand the term more. Perhaps there will be some statistics about different countries and their carbon footprints – you might be curious to see which country is top of the carbon-neutral list and wonder how they have managed to achieve that. Expand your knowledge until your curiosity is satisfied.

IN A PAIR

Have a conversation about anything: your day, what your school was like, your favourite clothes – anything. One of you speaks, the other listens. However, the listener can interrupt to redirect the conversation based on their curiosity. Get your partner to expand on topics that interest you, from as many different angles as possible. For example:

> **Person A:** Normally for breakfast I have cereal but today I had ...
>
> **Person B:** Has that been for your whole life? Having cereal?
>
> **Person A:** No, well – maybe when I was a teenager and then I started eating it again about two years ago.
>
> **Person B:** Do you have a favourite cereal?
>
> **Person A:** Mostly I eat muesli to be healthy but I have a secret stash of Coco Pops that no one else knows about. We weren't allowed them as kids so now I have them to defy my parents.
>
> **Person B:** Why do you think your parents wouldn't let you have Coco Pops?

You get the idea. **Person B** is getting **Person A** to expand around cereal because the way **Person A** mentioned cereal made them curious (the word 'normally' perhaps drew attention to a routine that **Person B** wanted to know more about).

This exercise is based on one I was taught by the fantastic community creator Ruth Moir, called Listening to Ignite. When

Ruth introduced me to this exercise I felt so grateful. It encourages us to not only listen with interest but to light up our partner, encourage them to deepen their story and let them know that we are not just curious, but that we are fascinated to hear what they have to say.

FAILURE

Fact: No one likes failure. It sucks. It hurts. You feel like an idiot. Often there is shame attached. We can tiptoe around, trying desperately not to fail but, unfortunately, it is a fact of life that we are all going to achieve some whopper failures in our lives as well as lots of tiny, tiny ones. A smorgasbord of failure, if you like. Failures, mistakes, hiccups all laid out on a platter for you to enjoy. We have to embrace failure, thank it for its teaching and stride into the world, looking to the scars failure has left us, for guidance. Failure may be hard, but it teaches us better ways to communicate, better ways to express ourselves and better ways to cope when things don't go the way we thought they would. I like the way director Peta Lily puts it when she says: 'Think of failure as a trampoline – a place you temporarily land on which will soon provide your next exhilarating up.' Well, let's get ready to bounce.

Retell Your Failure Story

Improv can only be learned through failure, which is why it is such great training. Every class you attend, you have to get it wrong, so you can feel what it feels like to get it right. It's like learning to ride a bike, but naked and in front of your peers. Everything is wobbling, including your ego.

The class is going to see all of you, and worse, they are going to see how you respond to failure. Once we know how we react when things don't go the way we thought they would, we can think about our relationship with failure.

Top five responses to failure in an improv class:

1. **The Blamer** – Points to the offer someone else made in the scene that ruined everything.
2. **The Hider** – Stands at the back of the scene and makes no offers to be sure not to be responsible for the failure.
3. **The Questioner** – Asks questions to figure out what happened, sits quietly and ponders on the answers. Might send a follow-up email.
4. **The Laugher** – Finds the mistakes hilarious, accepting responsibility and brushing it off all at once. Sometimes a little too quickly.
5. **The Apologiser** – Reaches deep into their soul to self-flagellate their terrible offers that ruined everything. The class cannot continue until they have received their peers' full forgiveness.

Perhaps you recognise some of these in yourself. The exciting thing about failure is you can respond in a variety of ways. I used to be a 5 followed by a 1 followed by a 3. Now I am a 3 followed by a 4 with the occasional 1 creeping in, for old times' sake.

Once we know how we respond to failure, we can decide if our response is serving us or not. When I started improv, I would apologise whenever I made a mistake, no matter how small. Often I would send long, weeping emails about how I felt I had ruined the show. These were often met with counter offers of ownership of mistakes made, a spiral of declarations that got increasingly ridiculous. It was exhausting.

I started to notice how similar my responses to improv failures were to real life failures. Performing is very generous in the amount of failure it allows you to experience, often in no uncertain terms. From shows that people have walked out of and lines I have forgotten mid-show to stand-up gigs where people cocked their head to the side and, instead of laughing, felt sorry for me*. I thought that every time a little thing went wrong, I was a massive failure.

It meant that each failure overwhelmed anything that could count as success. The gigs that went well, the shows when I was word-perfect and the audiences that stayed to watch right till the end. No wonder I felt like I was failing, I wasn't allowing myself to see any of my successes.

I had made my failing personal: that I was a failure, rather than I had failed. A subtle but lethal difference. If you start to believe you are a failure rather than the events or projects

---

* Quite literally the worst. Booing and heckling are nothing compared to an audience who are concerned about the choices you've made in life. Once a man followed me out of a gig where I died on my arse and said, 'Don't worry, I thought you were pretty good. What's your real job?' He was unable to hide his horror when I said, 'This. I am a comedian.' BURN.

themselves are failing, it becomes impossible to objectively disentangle what is in your control and what is out of your control.

Internal vs External

There are internal and external factors involved in any failure. Those we can control (internal) and those we cannot (external). We are back to Epictetus again.

In performance, the external factors are huge. The amount of chance that goes into any career, let alone a showbiz one, is enormous, but I wasn't able to see that yet. I thought it was all part of a divine plan. Do enough auditions and your time will come. In the fantastic book, *The Biggest Bluff*, psychologist and poker player Maria Konnikova notes: 'We don't often question the role of chance in the moments it protects us from others or ourselves. When chance is on our side, we disregard it: it is invisible. But when it breaks against us, we wake to its power. We begin to reason the whys and hows.'

Chance is perhaps the greatest of the external variables working alongside a performer. But it is true in every facet of life. Your business is reliant on the economy and it crashes = not your fault. You drive into another car because they brake suddenly = not your fault*. You are about to take the kids to school and one loses a shoe and the other reminds you that they are supposed to arrive dressed as their favourite Egyptian

---

* Unless you were changing the radio station at the time.

pharaoh. You turn up at the school gates and all the other parents look at your bedraggled self, one child wearing a pyramid hat shaped out of tin foil and you think: 'Have I failed as a parent?' No! The world just bombarded you with new information and you only had three minutes to improvise your way out of it. Congratulations on your tin foil skills.

Once I auditioned to play the part of a vacuum cleaner and I didn't get it. It was the millionth rejection I had had and it was the straw that broke the camel's back. I thought: 'What am I? How can I call myself an actor if I can't even get the part of an inanimate object?' It wasn't even a Dyson. It was just a bog standard vacuum cleaner in a children's TV show. I stopped auditioning for a while after that. It wasn't even the vacuum cleaner so much as the slow grind of being told NO over and over again. I felt like such a massive failure. I needed to clean up my act.

I wasn't yet able to see the external factors because I was too fixed on the internal. I let the rejection get to me. I took it to heart. I thought they were rejecting me rather than the fact I wasn't right for the job. I stopped believing in myself. I created conspiracy theories in my head – everyone in the industry hates me. It was easier to believe a big, convoluted story where every casting director in the UK had conspired that I should never work in TV, rather than the actual truth – I just wasn't right for these parts. I wasn't the vacuum cleaner they were looking for.

Balance

We have to keep in balance why the thing in question failed. Looking to the external only, without including the internal, does not lead to growth. If we always blame others for our failing, we will never grow. If we only look internally for what went wrong, if we only blame ourselves, we cannot move forward. We must return to the notion of curiosity. Let the pain subside, cry or scream if you need to, and then do a gentle investigation into what went wrong.

One weekend around the time of the vacuum cleaner incident, I was doing some gigs in Paris with two much older male comics*. One of them was so sunny and delightful and the other was this bitter, miserable guy who just kept moaning about how he wasn't famous and no one ever gave him any chances. He went on and on for the whole weekend.

He continued moaning all the way into the lift at our hotel. Myself and the other (up until this point quite quiet) comic were staying on the same floor, which meant our moaning friend got out a floor before. When the doors closed, the other comic turned to me and said, 'Oh god, he doesn't half moan, does he?' I laughed and said how it must be hard not to get bitter in this industry. He turned to me and he said, 'You know,

---

*This was very normal. It probably still is quite normal. If you are a young woman on the club circuit, you spend a lot of time with older dudes. I had many hilarious times but occasionally you just wanted someone you could discuss tampons with.

once I was given my own TV show. It had my name in the title and everything. It was signed off and I was walking on air. The next month, the commissioner changed. My show was taken away from me – they decommissioned it. I didn't even know you could do that.'

'That must have been horrible.' I said.

'It was. But you know what, Pippa? It was just one thing. Sure, it hurt like hell, but I still get to do what I love every day. I perform around the world. I have a family who love me. What more could I want?'

And with that, he got out of the lift. It was so ludicrously clear, it was like the universe decided to show me the two paths I could take. I could sit and stew in my failure, get bitter and shout at the world for the rest of my life, or I could put it down to a life experience, use it to grow and go on my way.

It wasn't a difficult decision.

Success for me was a very narrow goal. With my eyes so fixed on auditions and accolades, I wasn't even noticing what I *was* doing. My perceived failure was not getting every part I auditioned for. My actual failure was not adapting my goals as I grew as a performer, as the goal posts changed, as my choices opened up and other paths became available. So, after I licked my wounds (and several pints of Häagen-Dazs), I shifted my focus from noticing the things I wasn't achieving to the things I was. I shifted my work focus to things that were fulfilling me: writing songs, improvising musicals and teaching. Most importantly, I shifted my definition of success to be values based, instead of appearance based. I would consider myself a success if I was doing what I loved doing, had time to invest in family and friends and my work had a greater purpose. I suddenly felt I was following my path. Most importantly, that feeling of failure went away. I haven't looked back.

Success Isn't So Pure

The idea of success started to bother me after a while. Not because we shouldn't have goals and aims, but because success no longer seemed to me a clean, clinical end point. Within everything that is deemed a success, failure has been there. Scientists thrive on failure to lead them to success. When a hypothesis is proved wrong, they are closer to finding what the answer they are looking for is, so they need to fail to succeed.

I am a big fan of the story of the Thames Tunnel. Not a sentence you might expect me to write in an improv book, but let me explain. It was the first tunnel ever to be built under a river and it was headed up by Marc Brunel, dad of Isambard (him with the tall hat from the Olympic opening ceremony). Between 1825 and 1843, teams of engineers and workers strived to create this unthinkable idea*. They failed many, many times. The soft London clay would fall away as they dug under the River Thames and the tunnel would flood. They ran

---

* I love the idea that at one point, tunnels seemed crazy. 'What is it? A long hole?' Now we don't even blink when we go through one, but these guys had to fight to build one.

out of money. People got sick from the exposure to sewage. People literally died so that we could have tunnels.

They plotted and dug and flooded and drained for 18 years, but eventually they did it: the first ever tunnel. The Thames Tunnel was opened to the public on the 25th of March 1843. Today, it is part of the Overground network of Transport for London. Most people won't realise, on their journey into town, that they are travelling through such a remarkable piece of history.

The Thames Tunnel is officially a success. But if we are to accept the Thames Tunnel was a success, we must accept that success contains failure. They made the first tunnel under a river. That is amazing. Standing ovation, Team Brunel. However, it was over budget, it took far longer than they planned (the project was in fact abandoned for seven years because they ran into financial issues) and people died. All these things are not to say we should never use tunnels again, but instead to notice the journey that was undertaken, the failures that had to be overcome to achieve this success. Failure is always a part of success.

Improv as Failure Training

The only way to learn improvisation is through failure. You stand up in front of a group of strangers and you give it a go. You cannot learn any other way. You can read all the improv books and watch all the YouTube tutorials, but until you are stood in front of people and putting yourself out there, you have not fully immersed yourself in improvisation.

The first rule of failure in improv and so in life: You have to be willing to fail.

This is true of pretty much everything. For example, dating. The entire process is built on failure. Meeting someone, going on a few dates and realising that it isn't working. In other words, you have to kiss a few frogs. How many of us have kept dating someone because we really want to be in a relationship, even though this one isn't going anywhere? We keep going, laughing at their jokes when they are really not funny, finding ways to brush over questionable opinions, reminding ourselves that whilst we may not feel excited to see them, they do have really nice hair. Let it fail. Let this relationship fail so you can take a breath and look at what wasn't right. If a date doesn't work out, it may be a failure in one sense, but it is also a nudge to find the person with whom you are more compatible.

The second rule of failure in improv and so in life: You have to acknowledge and work with mistakes, including your own.

'There are no mistakes in improv' is a common adage. I would like to modify it to: 'The only mistake in improv is how we respond to potential mistakes.' Sometimes an improviser walks into a scene and says something that makes no sense. They have not been listening to what went before, or they missed a vital piece of information, or they panic and words tumble out of their mouth before they can stop them. Perhaps you are doing a scene set in a gothic castle and another performer comes in and says: 'Four pints of Stella please.' You have set it up to be medieval times, yet here is an offer from modern times. You can't stop the show, so you need to work with what they say and make it part of the tapestry of the scene.

'Ah yes, my liege. I am so glad Lord Wetherspoon was able to save our gothic architecture and turn it into one of his low-cost taverns.'

Nailed it.

This is great practise in humility. You've set up a lovely scene and your friend, the improviser, comes in and offers a curveball. It's done now. Once that offer is out of their mouth, they can't take it back. So you can pretend it didn't happen (despite the fact everyone knows it's been said) or you can YES AND it to the high heavens and see where it takes you. It is the YES AND attitude that turns a potential 'mistake' into a vital offer. The way the mistake is handled stops the impro-viser feeling like a failure and the show from failing.

In life there are times when people throw us a curve ball and we have to acknowledge it (YES) and then decide how to move forward (AND). In situations when you are presenting a united front, this is especially important. Someone reveals new information during a meeting that you were unaware of and you have to choose how to incorporate it into the plan you have already made. Your partner reveals that you are moving house to your mother-in-law's and now you have to pretend it wasn't a big secret. Perhaps you arrange for a friend to come for dinner and when they arrive, they inform you that they are on a special diet that means they cannot eat fish or dairy. You look at the fish pie you made with all the love in your heart. Frustrating – although you didn't check in with them if they had any restrictions and they are known for chopping and changing their diet. If we go back to those top five responses to failure, we can imagine how we might best respond. You can get angry with them, spend the time arguing about whose responsibility it was to get the dietary information, or you can show them what they could have won, whilst you whip them up a nice bowl of brown rice and broccoli*. Next time, hopefully they'll remember to offer this info up in advance and you'll remember to ask.

Third rule of failing in improv and so in life: Take your learning back on stage with you, not your pain.

When improvisers first start out, those shows that fail are so painful. The audience stare, dead-eyed, wondering what they paid for. You can feel the shame burn while you are on stage. You look to the clock and there is still 30 minutes to go. When the show is finished, the audience can't look you in the eye as they walk by you in the bar. It is horrific. 'Don't be silly, it's just an improv show!' well-meaning muggle friends will say, but we put our heart and soul on the line and it didn't pay off. That hurts.

For this, I go to the fabulous comedian Sarah Millican and quote her '11 o'clock rule':

This is Millican's Law. If you have a hard gig – quiet, a death, a struggle, whatever – you can only be mad and frustrated and gutted until 11am the next day. Then you must draw a line

---

* I know what I'd rather eat.

*under it and forget about it. As going into the next gig thinking
you are shit will mean you will die.*

*Equally, if you nail it, slam it, destroy it, whatever, you can
only be smug about it until 11am the next day (in the past, I
have set an alarm so I could get up and gloat for an extra half
hour) as if you go into the next gig thinking you are God's gift
to comedy, you will die. That is Millican's Law and it totally
works. It means you move on quickly.*

This is such a helpful rule for performance and whilst we
may not be able to take it directly into life (some knocks are
more complicated to process than having a few chips thrown
at you at a gig above a pub) the idea that we need to feel the
failure and then move past it is vital. We need to have a better
relationship with failure and that includes how we process
the emotions that come with it. They are uncomfortable. We
will try to push past them. Squash them down, only to replace
them with anger towards an external source or feign indiffer-
ence about the experience. If we don't process, we can't get
past it.

Process, then pass.

Is Failure Worth It?

Life without failure sounds pretty idyllic, right? Gliding from
place to place, never worrying about anything. The truth is, to
grow as a human, we have to fail. Watch kids learn to walk –
they fall on their bums and get back up. Imagine they just

gave up after the first try? They cry and get frustrated, but they keep getting up. Kids try things; they explore and they fail constantly. As adults, we lose this sense of curiosity, the fearlessness of trying. The consequences loom too large.

I love Brené Brown's book, *Daring Greatly*. She asks: 'What's worth doing even if I fail?' This is a fantastic question to take into life. This relationship is worth investing in even if it fails, or this job, this protest, this project. Reaching for perfection is no use. Discovering the pattern as we go, finding perfection in what emerges. For that which emerges is the perfection we seek. We just didn't know it looked like that.

When We Are Failed

A part of the failure family that is hard to process is not when we fail, but when we are failed. When someone or something lets us down. When we experience giving our everything, only for our offer to be ignored, repeatedly. Perhaps you have been failed by your parents, your workplace or community, and it floored you. To be failed is painful and can break that oh so important life force – trust. A parent with a mental health issue was not able to look after you in the way you needed. Your boss wilfully chose not to put you up for a promotion, whilst telling you they were backing you all the way. A friend did not defend you when you were being attacked.

The only choice we have in these moments is over how we respond, and the most important and hardest part of that response for most of us is forgiveness. We can get so stuck in resentment and revenge, that we are unable to move forward. Yet forgiveness is the first step to moving forward. It does not mean that we accept their behaviour, rather that we choose not to be held back by their failure of us any longer. When we hold that anger inside us, it is possible that we will allow their failure to destroy us. Though it may take time, it is possible to be failed, to forgive and to move on.

Do Not Let Fear of Failure Stop You

Fear of failure will stop us doing things. Stop us making friends. Stop us speaking out. Stop us stepping forward. Stop us. Practise failing every day. Make it something that teaches you rather than tortures you because failure is always with us. It's that friend who always says the thing you don't want to hear. Sometimes you wonder why you are friends with her, but you know she'll always tell you the truth.

Next time you fail: recover, reflect and get ready to fail again.

Exercise Corner

SOLO

Let's do an experiment. Choose a part of your body that you might like to get an imaginary tattoo on. Now think about all the times you have failed and what those tattoos might say. If you love to draw, take some time and draw your failure tattoo. They can be as specific as you like. Mine would have the following:

1. A toilet cubicle for the time I bitched about my boss in the bathroom and she was in the cubicle next door.
2. A broken heart for all my failed relationships.
3. An ear full of cotton wool for all the times I failed to listen.
4. An awkward smile emoji for all the times I didn't know what to say when someone was in pain.
5. Some closed eyes for when I ignored something I didn't want to deal with.

Got all your tattoos? Now I want you to move this on a step and think about what you learned from each one of those failures. So mine would be:

1. Don't bitch. But if you do, check the person isn't in the toilet.
2. So many different learnings; value yourself more, being handsome does not excuse everything, sometimes it's just the wrong time.

3. Listen better. Pay attention. Put down your phone.
4. You don't have to always say something, just be with them.
5. These things don't go away. Open your eyes and deal with it or you'll carry it around forever.

With these imaginary tattoos, once you can see clearly what you have learned, the tattoo will start to fade. It may not disappear completely, but it will not be so bright as when you first got inked. Perhaps it needs to stay for a little longer. It takes time to learn from our failures and the bigger the mistake or the more painful the failure, the longer that tattoo might remain.

IN A PAIR

Take a tennis ball and play, 'can't catch'. You throw the ball to each other and you must make the biggest effort to catch the ball and then fail. Dive for it and miss. Leap for it. Enjoy not catching the ball.

Now take it in turns to tell each other your failure stories and invite the other to retell it as a story of learning. I take this from a class I was teaching where I invite people to tell their life stories to each other and have them retold as fairy tales. One man burst into tears at his retelling because his partner talked about the adversity that this man had overcome to arrive where he was today. This man had never thought of it like that. He told the class: 'I felt such shame about that period in my life and yet here, just being told my story back as a moment of learning, I feel released.' It was very beautiful.

Don't let your failure stories own you. You own them. They are a part of you and not the whole of you.

Ten Improv Tips

Students often ask me if there are any tricks that they can use in everyday life and, of course, there are. I have them right here in my purse. Here are ten tips* for quick fixes.

1. **Eyebrows Up!**
   My first improv teacher, Alan Marriott, taught me this, and I have never forgotten it. Before you go into a scene, raise your eyebrows, as it counteracts the thinking furrowed brow. So if you find yourself starting to go down a spiral of anxiety or panicked working it all out, just raise your eyebrows and the world seems a little bit lighter.

2. **Clear Strong Offers**
   Often, we are misunderstood because our offer wasn't clear. When making offers – when asking for something – be as clear as you possibly can. The weaker our offer, the easier it is to get mistaken. So if you want to arrange dinner with a pal, it will be easier if you say, 'Let's meet at 7 o'clock on Friday' than, 'Some time next week'. A strong offer can be accepted, rejected or negotiated with much more easily. 'I love you' is easier to understand than, 'I think I quite like you'. 'I'll have a pint of beer' is clearer

---

* Tips is what hacks used to be called. I prefer the word tip because it feels less aggressive. I don't think life is something you need to hack. It is not an international fraud conspiracy and we are not Gus Gorman.

than, 'Oh you choose, I don't mind' unless you really don't mind. Just don't be upset when they come back from the bar with a watermelon Bacardi Breezer.

3. **Take a Breath**

Before responding to anything, take a breath. It will allow the words in a conversation to land with you and give space for you to respond rather than react. Practise with small things like ordering a burger at Maccy D's (how often have you ended up with not quite the right thing because you felt pressured to order and went with the McChicken sandwich, again) and then see if you can bring it in during a conversation with a friend or a partner when you are discussing something more sensitive. Particularly useful when someone is annoying you, even though they aren't doing anything officially wrong.

4. **Voice Mirror**

Sometimes, if I am tired and zoning out in conversations or whilst listening to a long talk, I use this technique to help me get back on top of what is being said. While the person is talking, you say exactly what they are saying, in your head. Exactly as you are doing now. Each of these words you can hear in your head* as if you are reading

---

* If you are listening to the audiobook, this is true in a different way. Imagine you are reading the book, not listening, and my voice that you are hearing is in fact your voice, reading it. I have made this far more complicated than it needs to be.

aloud. You can practise on a YouTube video – watch a Ted Talk and repeat each word, in your head, as it is spoken. Eventually you will be so in tune you will be able to finish their . . .

5. **Look Everyone in the Eyes**

This is for when you might have to address a crowd. When I was working with Ken Campbell, the theatre maverick (you might recognise him from 'The Anniversary' episode of 1970s TV show, *Fawlty Towers**), he would say, 'Make sure you have looked every single member of the audience in the eyes at least once by the end of the performance.' It is one of the best tricks I have ever learned. You feel connected to the audience – they feel seen and they become less frightening, as they are now just a room full of friendly people, looking rather than an audience, staring.

6. **Check Your Face**

Every so often, bring your attention to your face. The demand is not that you have a Cheshire Cat grin, constantly planted across your face, but that you are not giving incorrect messages to your compadres because you are lost in thought or concentrating hard. Your face may not be making the facial expression that corresponds with how you are actually feeling.

---

* If your DVD collection is as old as mine. DVD? Who am I kidding? I still have it on VHS. Retro cool or stuck in the past? You decide.

7. **Don't Judge Someone by Their Face**

They are probably thinking about their dinner.

8. **That Reminds Me . . .**

I love using this when in conversation. If you struggle to chat at parties, use the phrase 'That reminds me . . .' to link into what is being talked about. So, if someone is talking about a holiday in Italy, what does that remind you of? Could be a whole story about a holiday you took, or a question about their holiday linked to a fact you remembered about spaghetti trees*.

9. **Be Present**

You don't have to talk to be part of a conversation. Just be present. Many improv scenes would be improved by people just listening and encouraging. The same can be said for most group conversations.

10. **You Can Leave the Scene**

Most improvisers, when they are first learning, find it impossible to leave scenes that are going nowhere. They stand there, floundering, trying to find the 'answer' to a scene that has no chemistry, content or joy. No one is demanding this scene happen, but we wade through the treacle, hoping the answer will emerge. The best choice is to LEAVE THE STAGE. It takes great courage to

---

* On 1 April 1957, the BBC broadcast a three-minute report of trees that grew spaghetti in Switzerland. Still the most incredible April Fool since time began.

know when something isn't working, that you have tried everything you can. Whether that is a conversation or a relationship, sometimes you just need to walk away.

EMPATHY AND THE ART OF NOT FIXING THINGS

A student takes to the stage in my improv class.

'All the money is gone!' they say to their partner, Nadine, writhing in torment. 'We'll have to sell everything, Nadine. The house, the car, the children – everything.' They start to cry and mime opening a bottle of wine, as if to drown their sorrows. Nadine looks at him and says 'Don't worry, Marlon, I've got all this money right here under the table. I knew this might happen.'

Marlon looks a little dumbfounded, but quickly responds with, 'I'm sorry, Nadine. I took that money and spent it too. I have a spending problem. Like Elton John. Only I don't have the budget of Elton John. Or the songwriting skills. So actually, it is a problem. All the money is gone!'

Nadine, in an attempt to make the problem go away, to remove the pain of her fellow character, pulls off her shoe and announces, 'That's why I always carry this cheque* my

---

* A cheque is an old way of paying for things. Imagine a ten pound note. Now imagine a piece of paper that you write '£10' on and sign. Shops used to accept that as payment! What a world.

grandmother wrote on her deathbed. I knew that 20 million pounds would come in handy!'

Marlon's shoulders sink. 'Oh, great. Well, problem solved.'

And the scene grinds to a halt.

This is the common issue in improv of 'fixing'. Plastering over the pain so that everything can and will be fine. We have an imaginary box of anything in improv, so surely we want to show the world as a pain-free Utopia? The answer is, no. Amazingly, the improv audience rarely wants joyful, happy endings. In children's shows*, sweet, shiny faced children routinely ask to see characters murdered, bullied and tortured. They want to see action and consequence, played out before them. At one show, 400 children demanded the death of every single character. We did exactly as they asked. All the actors died (we were playing mountaineers and each of us froze or lost our footing or fought a snow-man who put icicles through our hearts). The narrator looked at the bodies on the stage and asked the children, 'Well now what?' A little hand was raised gingerly and a questioning voice said, 'They come back to life?' Now the extremes of life, death and consequences had been explored in the story, the children realised they preferred a world where everyone wasn't dead.

———————————

* Children are by far the best audience for improvisation as they have no interest in being clever but rather wish to push the grown-ups to explore what is possible. I cannot tell you how many times I have had to do a hundred cartwheels, dance like a monkey or have my head explode. They take great joy in seeing the impossible manifest in five grown-ups wearing colourful dungarees.

The audience are happy to watch action and consequence, but the improviser often struggles to deliver this. When Marlon enters at the top of the example scene, it is clear he wants to explore his misery at having lost all the money. Nadine, the actor, is keen to wrap up the incident and keep things chipper. This will be a subconscious action – Nadine will not know she has done this, but with her wish to resolve the external plot quickly, she has not left space to explore what is happening in the moment in Marlon's inner world.

When I asked Nadine what she thought she was doing in that scene, she said, 'I was accepting Marlon's offer* – he needed money, and I gave him the money. I YES ANDed the problem.' Well yes, and no. By accepting and then immediately removing the problem, they are actually changing the offer. The offer is, 'I have ruined everything,' but solving the problem immediately makes the scene say: 'Money is not an issue for us.' There is a negation of the emotional offer from Marlon. He doesn't get to process feeling bad about having no money. That reality is taken away from him, rather than worked through. Instead of YES AND-ing the problem (there is no money), this is a time to YES AND the emotion (fear and distress). We are confusing 'problem' and 'offer.' We do this in life all the time.

----

* A reminder that 'offer' means the reality within which we are working or that which our partner has brought to us. It is anything tangible that can be worked with to give texture to the scene.

Fixing in the Real World

An improvised scene, of course, is not reality. If a friend came to you in real life and said, 'I think I'm going to lose my house,' it is unlikely you would be able to help them pay their mortgage, no matter how much you would like to*. But in a wish to take our friend's pain away, we might start offering solutions. We put our brownie guide, best-foot-forward hat on and try to solve the problem. We scour the internet and send links to possible solutions – short term loans, an article by that money guy off *This Morning*, a special incense that is supposed to bring you luck, rather than sitting with our pal and letting them work through their sorrow, their frustration, their anger. Because it is uncomfortable. Especially if we are OK when our friend is not. Instead of letting our friend explore how they are feeling about the situation, how wretched it is to not be able to provide for your family, how terrifying the prospect of losing your home is – we tend to want to move them straight to action, so we don't have to think about how horrible it might be for us to be in that situation. We might feel guilt at our reverse situation, sadness that we cannot take away our friend's pain. That is hard to sit in, but I invite you to.

The idea that if there is a problem, we must immediately find the solution, is a modern conundrum. In days gone by there would be wailing, rituals, prayers. We would tell our

---

* If you do have the ability to pay off people's mortgages, please DM me.

community our woes and they would light a candle for us. But now, as we have lost connection to what might be called 'spiritual practices' we prefer life hacks to soul searching. It is easier to fix a problem than to feel it – the discomfort of it. In the improv scene at the beginning of the chapter, Nadine is helping Marlon by not having him go through the pain of losing everything, but in doing so has denied Marlon a part of himself, his pain and ultimately his ability to heal. They have not been able to work through their emotional offer, the problem has been solved without a connection to their inner world. Our characters are left with a practical solution but not an emotional resolution. In fixing the problem immediately, we have taken away discovering the solution connected in both practical and emotional truth. We deal with the physical problem but not the trauma, which is not satisfying for the performers or the audience. Imagine if they did this in soap operas:

> **Sandy:** I can't believe you are having an affair with that singer!
> **Fern:** I do apologise. I have deleted her number and booked us – you and I – a holiday to reconnect.
> **Sandy:** Ok, thanks. Pop-Tart®?
> **Fern:** No – she was into jazz*.

The audience at home would be in uproar. People would be tweeting in like crazy:

---

* Ba dum tish!

@SoapOpera There's no way they would move on that
    quick!

@SoapOpera Are these people robots? That is going to
    come back to haunt them.

@SoapOpera Excellent Pop-Tart® joke but other than
    that, Sandy and Fern are gonna have ISSUES!

Fixing things is a great way to avoid the emotional load of
them. We are obsessed with conflict resolution being a quick,
painless process rather than a slow, nuanced journey. The joy
of narrative improv exercises is: we can practise exploring
these difficult situations in a fictional world, so that we might
come back into our 'real' world and find this work less alien
and less daunting, if not less painful.

Imagine you are taking part in a marathon*. You have done
all the training. You've bought the equipment. You've done
your #FirstMarathon selfie on Insta and your family is all waiting at the finish line to celebrate when you're done. You
mention to your running buddy that you are nervous, and
your buddy says, 'Don't worry – I've got my car around the
corner. We can drive to the end and no one will know.' In many
ways this is the perfect solution – you don't have to get
exhausted running the race and you still get the glory of crossing the finishing line. You accept.

The start gun goes off – you both make a show of the first
half a mile and then get in the car when no one is looking.

---

* I will never run a marathon as they seem completely pointless to me.
Twenty-six miles is a long way to run just to destroy the cartilage in your
knees. Analogy still works though.

Your buddy has a tray of Krispy Kremes waiting for you. You chomp them down and enjoy the naughtiness of the drive, leaping out 100 yards before the end of the race. Doing great 'tired running' acting, you cross the finish line in pretty good time (you waited for a few people to win, you aren't stupid). Your family rushes to congratulate you. Your mum tells you it's your greatest achievement* and to top it all off, your niece presents you with a tray of Krispy Kremes. 'You deserve them,' they all say, with a big, toothy grin. You didn't get to do the work, so your feelings are displaced. Instead of feeling victorious, you feel guilty.

All actions have emotional responses. Your running buddy was trying to help you, but they have stopped you feeling a real sense of achievement – of going through the ups and downs of running a marathon, the trials of running all that way. So whilst the end goal has been met, the emotional journey hasn't. And so, you are not satisfied. Also, you never want to see a Krispy Kreme again.

Fixing Stops Empathy

Personally, it has taken me a long time to recognise my fixing tendencies. The intention is coming from a good place: I wish to stop anyone from having to struggle or feel pain. You are having trouble writing a song? I'll write it for you! You are really pissed off with your mother? Let me remind you of all

---

* Bit harsh.

the great things about her so I can cancel out your rage. You have lost your job? Let me tell you about four opportunities I have found for you in the last ten minutes, just by Googling 'Jobs in Luton'. All of these actions are of noble intention but stifling in reality.

My friend had a miscarriage. She and her partner were very sad, having hoped for a family for so long. I gave them a hug and said I was sorry and then followed it up with, 'At least you now know you can get pregnant.' I might as well have started singing, 'Always Look on the Bright Side of Life', for what I was really saying was, 'Don't be sad right now.' I could feel I hadn't said the right thing. There was an awkward silence, and my friend, knowing I am not an arsehole said, 'We aren't there yet,' and I said, 'Sorry'. For that is all we can do when we get these things wrong. Apologise and spend some time learning from the error.

I thought I was being helpful. Pointing out a silver lining they couldn't see. How horrified I was when researching empathy to find that Brené Brown, the great sociologist and author of *Daring Greatly*, uses that same example of a response* to a friend's miscarriage in her 'Empathy vs Sympathy' video for the Royal Society of the Arts. 'Empathy fuels connection. Sympathy drives disconnection.' Brown says. If we want to practise empathy we need to be able to take on our friend's perspective, without judging them and recognise the emotion that they are sitting with. Then we sit with them in that

---

* Not my personal example, but the same situation. I don't think Brené Brown is looking at my WhatsApp messages.

emotion and make space for whatever needs to emerge. As Brown says: 'Rarely can a response make something better. What makes something better, is connection.'

Fixing the presented problem without letting it have space to breathe doesn't deal with underlying emotions or issues, it just pushes them down, deep into our bellies. Because what we actually want to talk about isn't usually the first thing that we present. 'I'm not getting on with my husband' is not me asking you to get rid of my husband or find us a hobby we can do together, it's actually me saying, 'I am scared of being alone,' or, 'I am really sad right now'. In narrative improvisation, we can work with these situations in a fictional sense, so that when we are faced with them in real life, they feel less alien. We can explore what we might say and how that might play out, in a space where there are no real-life consequences.

Using Narrative Improv to Explore Empathy

In narrative improv*, the actors don't know what issues the characters are going to have at the start of the show – they reveal themselves throughout the story. This means that we will be presented unexpectedly with emotional moments and must discover how our characters navigate them. This is also true for the audience.

---

* By 'narrative improv' I mean a story rather than short, unrelated scenes. A show where the audience really get to know and invest in our characters.

Yet we cannot explore these moments if the other improvisers keep talking and doing 'business'. If the other improvisers keep focusing on making the next plot move or solving the problem of another character, rather than responding to the emotional offers and having an emotional response themselves. In such moments, the improviser simply needs to be present and attend to the other performer. Then there is space for the characters to truly connect.

Improvisation is a brilliant teacher of empathy because we get to play multiple people and see the world from their perspectives. It also means that we can practise playing a sympathetic character, an unsympathetic character, a cold character or a character who wants to empathise but doesn't know how. We can explore all these human facets in a fictional world where no harm can be done, so that when a situation presents itself that we might need to access empathy, it is easier to find. This doesn't always have to be done through huge, weighty scenes. Two frogs might discuss how hard it is when the tadpoles grow up; a fork could explain their rage at losing their knife partner to another fork.

Psychologists Thalia R. Goldstein and Ellen Winner backed this up in their study of young people who had spent more than a year in some kind of actor training: 'The tendency to become absorbed by fictional characters and feel their emotions may make it more likely that experience in acting will lead to enhanced empathy off stage.' I don't think it too much of an extension then to suggest that the improvisational aspect will add a further development here – enabling the actor an extra string which is to leap into any perspective with less fear, having become practised in the art of taking on characters instantly. We can rotate our view to another angle and stand in the shoes of our friend, our colleague or our fellow human.

Making up Solutions vs Discovering Them

When we talk about plot points in stories, we are talking about an incident or decision that happens, that leads to the next incident or decision. Person goes to shop and buys a pen, pen explodes, person returns to shop and gets a refund. Four plot points there – perhaps not the most exciting story, but we see 'thing happens which leads to next thing'.

During our *Showstopper!* rehearsals, it became clear that if we thought up those plot points in the scene as good plot points that worked intellectually but were not rooted in the emotional drive of the characters, the story was not nearly as satisfying to the audience or the improvisers as it was when the plot points were discovered in the moment, through character choices. When the characters were driven to a plot point through their relationship with either each other or the situation, the audience could understand how the character ended up where they were.

The AMC series, *Breaking Bad*, is brilliant for studying this because the characters make such wonderful, terrible choices. If you haven't seen the show, it is about a chemistry teacher, Walter White, who becomes a meth cook to pay for his cancer treatment*. Every decision Walter White makes, we see exactly how that moment comes to happen. We might not like it, or agree with it, but it makes a kind of sense, because each decision chimes with their emotional situation. When Walter kills a drug dealer in the basement, it is not pleasant, but we know why he does it. Then we watch him suffer for it, which leads to his next terrible decision. When we drive our story through emotional connection coupled with personal logic, each decision resonates with us far more than if we simply do as we are told or as we think we must.

Is It Always Bad to Fix Things?

If your friend comes round and asks to borrow a hammer to fix their broken door, you don't need to sit them down and hold their hand while they explain how the door got broken. You can give them a hammer and send them on their way. If your friend comes round to borrow a hammer and they are weeping about how their life is a mess, then you might want to go down the empathy route. Chances are, this visit isn't really about the hammer. If your friend wants to tell you, it'll be time for empathy. If they don't, give them the hammer and make sure they know the door is always open (and not because it is broken).

Fixing things is a way to make ourselves feel better by making our friend feel better, but it is often the opposite of

---

* If ever there was a show to make you grateful for the NHS, it is this one.

what is needed. Notice if you fix things for people and check in if it is always necessary. Maybe your friend just wants a hug, or a person to share their pain with. Whatever it is, we'll never get to the bottom of it if we immediately put a plaster over it. Give space and leave the first aid box to the side, until it is needed.

Exercise Corner

SOLO

Find a news story that involves a few different points of view. Imagine yourself in the shoes of each of the people involved. How easy is it for you to see the story from everyone's point of view? This is different from asking you to agree with each of the viewpoints, but rather have some idea of what it might be like to be coming at the incident from their angle. If there is an angle you cannot understand, try to delve into why their viewpoint is hard for you to fathom.

IN A PAIR

In an attempt to know what we might want to say in a situation, we are going to do some reverse work or use via negativia*, by imagining everything we would not want to say.

For example, if my brother's wife had left him, I wouldn't say:

- Of course she has. We never understood why she married you in the first place.
- Another man, was it?
- Count yourself lucky, she was minging.

---

*Via negativia: a fancy way of describing the process of discovering what something is, by exploring what it is not.

In a pair, one of you will be a friend coming to you with their problem. Choose one of the lines below or come up with your own. The person pretending to be the receiver of the problem must think of the worst thing you could say in response.

- My boyfriend just broke up with me.
- Everyone forgot my birthday.
- My grandma died.
- I didn't get the job.

Now repeat the exercise with the same scenarios and think about what you might want to say. Put yourself in their shoes and feel empathy for the person. How can you be with them in your response?

WHAT'S YOUR STORY?

Telling Our Stories

Humans love a story. Since the beginning of time, we have shared tales around the fire, warned each other about the perils of the outside world and enjoyed a sneaky gossip or two. Red Riding Hood taught us not to go into the woods alone and Mr Darcy taught us that not all men are the pricks they immediately seem*. To those of you who say you cannot tell stories: Piffle, I say. Piffle! Telling stories is the culmination of all the work we have been doing in this book. It might be happy, it might be sad, it might be both of those things and more. You have the tools to tell your stories now, we just need to put them all together.

Within all our lives, there are many, many stories. Things that have happened to us. We are sitting in our one, big storyline (life) which has a beginning (being born) a middle (living) and an end (death). Yet within that main story, there are many smaller stories happening. Imagine opening up your chest and revealing a whole library of books, each one containing a story

---

* Remember – some are.

from your life. Jobs you have worked, people you have loved, scrapes you've been in. Some stories have already been and gone, some you are in the middle of, some are yet to occur.

When we meet, we are often asked to tell a story about ourselves:

'What have you been up to?'

'Where did you grow up?'

'How do you know Ryan*?'

Telling a story about some aspect of our life is sharing a piece of ourselves with one another. We are giving our audience, the listener, a bit of our truth. This lays the foundation for trust: when we open up to each other – when we allow ourselves to be vulnerable – we connect. There is something conspiratorial about sharing our stories – we want to be known to each other and we want to know the worlds around us.

Despite this deep wish to share some of ourselves, the most common fear that appears in class is, 'I'm not good at telling stories,' or, 'I haven't really done anything interesting in my life.' So the first thing we are going to concentrate on in this chapter is how to take a life experience and construct the story we want to tell about it.

Let me reassure you about one thing: people are nosey – we love hearing about people's lives. What you think is dull

---

* If you are crashing a party, make sure you have this story prepped and ready to go. Best to go with vague but detailed here – 'He bought a top from me on eBay,' or, 'They got our orders mixed up in Burger King and we stayed in touch.' Then, immediately ask, 'How about you?' to get the attention away from you as you drink as many free drinks as you can before you get thrown out.

will be gold for many. I once sat next to a man who spent 45
minutes talking about how he got interested in panes of glass.
Forty-five minutes! And I was entranced. As a boy, he'd
wondered why he couldn't hear the road outside in one room
in his house but could in another. It turned out it was to do
with the curvature of the pane. Who knew it was possible to
have a lifelong love affair with the curvature of glass? This
guy did. It was the life he lived. And I lapped it up. If it had
been a book in his library, it would have been called *Glassy
Eyed**.

There are so many of these stories in our lives. Moments
of learning, humour, sadness. If I had to name some of the
stories in the library of my life, there would be *Visiting Great
Aunt Nellie*, *The Boy Who Broke My Heart* and *Vomiting in My
Fiancé's Armpit*. Have a think about your own life now – what
would be the titles of the stories you might write? These
stories don't need to be 45 minutes long. Nor do they need to
be perfect anecdotes. We just need to know why we are telling
them, and usually it's because they mean something to us.
They were a moment of change, of growth or total and utter
embarrassment. When we share these moments, the listener
sees themselves in your story and experiences a little of how
you see the world. Gathering perspectives is an important
part of our development from the single to the multiple view
that enables us to embrace the world fully, in all its complex
glory. So, first thing's first: let's get you confidently telling
some of your fabulous stories.

----

* *"Takes a bow."*

Creating Basic Stories

Stories, in their simplest form, have a beginning, a middle and an end.

> I woke up and had a shower. (Beginning)
> There was no shampoo, so I used soap on my hair. (Middle)
> I now look like my hair is made of felt. (End)

It's not the greatest tale ever told, but it's a story. A bit of action with the shampoo. A bit of external change. A short story about the perils of shower supplies, if you will. When I am teaching story to a class of improvisers, I always start with the idea that the story should be pretty mundane, removing any expectation that someone's first improvised story should be a classic, to be repeated down generations of improvisers. It is imperative when starting improvised storytelling that we are OK with mediocre and dull stories. Once we can recognise a boring story, we can start to work towards a more interesting or satisfying one. To start with though, my friends, let's be dull.

Have a go for yourself. Write yourself a simple story about yourself in three lines:

Beginning –

Middle –

End –

How did you do? Does it feel like a complete story? If not, go back and check that you set the scene in the first line, something happens in the second line and you resolve it in the third. Remember, we aren't being interesting yet. We are just working on a little bit of structure.

The Circle of Ideas

Improv is often thought of as limitless, which it teaches us to be. However, limits can be helpful when creating. Knowing there is a boundary. If there is no boundary, the story can go on forever. If we want something that is finite, we are going to need some boundaries.

The Circle of Ideas is a brilliant visual for when we are creating a story (another gift from the mind of Keith Johnstone). When any new story begins, you have a massive circle that could hold any ideas, the size of the universe, so big you cannot truly imagine it. As the story progresses, as it becomes clearer what this story is about, the smaller that circle becomes. Like a net catching all the relevant ideas for you. For example, I say: 'I am going to tell you a story' – the only thing in the Circle of Ideas, currently, is the fact that you are going to get a story. Then I say: 'It is about my brothers' – the story circle has just shrunk a bit. If it is about my brothers, then we can take most non-brother related things out of the circle. 'It is about my brothers and the time we tried to dig to Australia.' The circle has shrunk even smaller. If I was to now go outside the Circle of Ideas, you – the listener – would be a little discombobulated.

You will have experienced the frustration of the Circle of Ideas not being adhered to, without even knowing it. Most commonly, when you are having a meeting about one thing – let's say your local neighbourhood committee is having a conversation about parking spaces – and someone wants to bring up another subject, let's say the bins. The bins might need to be talked about, but they are outside of the Circle of Ideas for this meeting. If you bring bins into it, you are widening the circle. If at the top of the meeting someone said, 'I know this meeting is about parking, but we really need to talk about the bins,' then perhaps the group would agree to expand the circle. However, if you are into the nitty gritty of whether you should have resident permit parking* and someone says, 'I really think we need to talk about the bins', then it is likely people will be frustrated that the agenda has been hijacked. The narrative has changed, and not for the better. For a more satisfying storytelling experience, respect the Circle of Ideas.

Story Shapes

Ever wondered why movies sometimes feel like you've seen them before, even though they are brand new releases? Why, even though you have never seen the film, you know the guy is going to go into that cave even though they told him not to, and he'll be saved by the unattractive-until-she-takes-her-glasses-off girl who he will marry, in the cave, at the end? It's

---

* Can you tell what we have been talking about in my area?

because we only have a finite amount of story shapes. In the same way they all have a beginning, middle and end, they also tend to fall into particular types of story, as illustrated by Christopher Booker in his book, *The Seven Basic Plots**. Christopher lists the story types (steeped in Jungian theory, if you want to chuck that into your dinner table patter) as the following:

- **Overcoming the Monster:** Hero defeats something or someone that wishes to destroy them – literally trying to kill them or maim their sense of self (think *Jaws*, *The Devil Wears Prada*).
- **Rags to Riches:** Unlikely person rises from adversity and obscurity to riches and notoriety (*Cinderella*, *Oliver Twist*).
- **The Quest:** Person goes on an epic adventure in search of an item or location, facing obstacles as they travel (*The Lord of the Rings*, *The Wizard of Oz*).
- **Voyage and Return:** Person goes to an often-fantastical land and returns home, full of experience (*Back to the Future*, *Gulliver's Travels*).
- **Comedy:** Hilarious and increasingly complicated chain of events which eventually leads to a clarifying event, meaning a happy end for most, if not all, characters (*Legally Blonde*, *Clueless*).
- **Tragedy:** Our main character (or 'protagonist') is flawed, unable to see their own flaws or rather, to escape them.

---

* But what's the book about, Chris?

When they meet their demise, brought about by their flaw, the audience feels sorry for them, seeing that they were not evil, but broken (*Taxi Driver*, *Macbeth*).

- **Rebirth:** Something occurs that causes our main character to change the way they live their life (*Beauty and the Beast*, *A Christmas Carol*).

Think of your favourite film – which category does it fit into? Unless you are into obscure arthouse cinema of the 1940s, chances are it will fit one of Booker's categories. Once you see it, you can't unsee it. Turn on Netflix and get ready to tick off your story types.

Within your own life, you have a version of all these stories. That is why they resonate and why it is so valuable to learn these shapes. I look back at my life and see so many chapters with these headings. *Overcoming the Monster* was definitely the tale of when I worked in a health food store and was constantly taken advantage of by the boss*. *Rebirth* was when I started going to church and gave my life to Jesus. *Rebirth 2: The Return* was when I left the church and started my own church for people who don't believe in God. So many stories, so little time.

Which story shapes speak to you? Can you think of a rags to riches moment or a time in your life where a character flaw stopped you from succeeding? Maybe a series of terrible dates that led to you meeting The One (or maybe you are still

---

* This sounds worse than it was. She just got me to do a lot of extra work without paying me a higher wage and I was too young to know my rights. Know your rights! Don't worry, I got her back by eating all the chocolate raisins in the storeroom.

in that story – good luck to you!). Take a moment to see if you can find these stories within your life story. These are your anecdotes. Stories you feel comfortable sharing with people because they contain a journey that you went on and you wish to impart your new found wisdom on others: whether that be, 'I just realised you've got to believe in yourself,' or, 'And that's why I don't go to that gym anymore'.

Give Us the Details

Most stories are not three lines long. To make a richer story – one that people want to listen to – we must expand the world we are creating. This, we at Showstopper, call 'Broadening' – detailing the setting and the characters so that they hold our interest. Introducing detail that tells us about the world we are entering and enabling our audience to see the world through their mind's eye.

How far should we broaden? Is there such a thing as too much detail? A good thing to remember is that there must be a reason for any detail brought in. So let's imagine you are telling a story about a date that went wrong. If that is the imaginary title, 'Bad Date', the fact that the restaurant you were in is in financial difficulty might not be a detail that is needed*. If you open a story with, 'I was on a date with this

---

* Unless that somehow affects the date; the restaurant shut down half-way through the meal or you had to eat standing up because they were burning all the furniture to keep warm.

lady called Eve and she was drop dead gorgeous, so gorgeous, in fact, I forgot how to speak', we, the audience, now expect to find out how you forgetting to speak affected the date and made it 'Bad'. If the story continues, 'It was interesting, actually, because the restaurant has closed down now', your audience will be left wondering whether this is a story about Eve or the restaurant. They are already expecting a comedy story shape, without knowing it, just from that first line. Now you seem to be giving them a tragedy about the restaurant industry. Stick to the details that will help you tell the story you have set up.

If there is a detail that feels particularly relevant, we can expand on it. In Showstopper, we call this 'Deepening'. We drill down into the juicy piece of story detail and get as much as we can from it. Let's explore this further, continuing with the 'Bad Date' story we began earlier.

'I was on a date with this woman called Eve and she was drop dead gorgeous, so gorgeous, in fact, I forgot how to speak. It was so embarrassing because normally I have so much to say, but I was so bedazzled by her big, brown eyes I literally stopped talking. My mouth dried up. I tried drinking water – so much water. She must have thought I had an obsession with the stuff. Every time she asked me a question, I tripped over my tongue. It wasn't even like she was asking me difficult questions. Just the standards, you know, "What do you do?" I couldn't even answer that. I literally forgot for a second and then when I tried to answer, all I managed to get out of my mouth was "Shops". One word!'

See how we are digging down into the details about Eve's beauty ('big, brown eyes'), the effect it had on the storyteller (embarrassed, panicking); these are the bits your audience are wanting to hear. Now all this story needs is a build to a climax (how bad can it get?) and then find an ending.

'She was trying to hide it, but I know she thought I was insane, which just made me get even more tongue-tied. I took another big gulp of water, but it went down the wrong way and I spat water out all over the table. She tried to not be disgusted, but I could see it in her beautiful eyes. After about an hour, with her doing most of the talking, she got a phone call – definitely one of those emergency "get your friend to call" phone calls – and said she had to leave because her friend was unwell. And so with one last chance to speak, I summoned all my courage to ask if I could see her again. I stood there, going red with anticipation and the only words that came out of my mouth, all loud and desperate were, "I love you!" I was horrified. Where did that even come from? The look she gave me. She just said, "Cool," and walked out of my life. I've never wanted the floor to swallow me up so badly. Now I practise speaking before I go on any date. Literally rehearse sentences like, "How are you?" "What do you do?" and, "Please don't leave."

The story has a beginning, a middle and an end. It builds to a climax of the storyteller blurting out, 'I love you,' and then resolves by Eve leaving and our storyteller never seeing them again. It fits into the comedy shape, and has enough detail that the people listening will be able to imagine it in their mind's eye. The listener will care about the storyteller because they have probably had a bad date experience, and they will want to hear how it ends because the set-up (beginning) has inferred something went wrong. The listener's curiosity will want to know what.

Have a go. Think of a story from your life and see how you can transform it into an anecdote. Which bits do you need to keep in and which do you need to leave out? Which story shape does it fit from the list? How can you mould it so it has a beginning, a middle and an end? How can you pique your audience's interest? What details are needed? The story doesn't have to be long, but it must have affected you in some way.

How Are You Telling Your Life Story?

When someone says, 'Tell me about yourself,' most of us aren't quite sure where to begin. Which parts of ourselves to highlight. Do we need to show off our accolades? Do they need to know about the time I got caught smoking at school or how I had a fling with a belly dancer last summer? Most of us, when asked about ourselves, tend to play our life experiences down. Telling our story like it isn't that interesting or that not much has happened in our lives.

A bit of this is not wanting the attention, a bit might be you don't want to tell this particular stranger your life story, but often, it's because we haven't given our story a lot of attention. So instead of thinking about what we might tell a stranger about our life, let's think about it this way: how do you tell yourself your life story?

We need to be able to tell our story to ourselves and see what we can learn from what has gone before. What events have shaped us, which moments have touched us and which experiences have scarred us. How do you think your story has gone so far? The angle from which we see our own story can affect how we move forward. If we look back and all we can see is failure, how is that affecting the way we might see our story continuing? If we only let ourselves hear our successes and try to cover up any moments of hardship, how will that affect our ability to face future challenges?

Here is one way to tell a well-known story:

'I wasn't very popular at school, and then, to top it all off, I got bitten by a radioactive spider and now I have no control over my life. Who am I? I can't even tell people about my superpowers. I am at the beck and call of a public who hate me. Also, I am constantly exhausted from climbing up buildings to catch criminals, which really isn't my job. Where are the police in all this?'

And another:

'I used to get bullied quite badly, but one day, I got bitten by a radioactive spider and now I have these amazing superpowers. I can climb up the outside of buildings and I save people's lives every day. It can be exhausting being a superhero, but I tell you, it is quite amazing knowing I have captured more villains in a month than the NYPD do in a year. At one point, I let my powers go to my head and it led to my uncle being murdered. It was then that I realised, with my powers came a responsibility. I found my purpose.'

Spiderman's life is pretty different in these two versions of his story. The first focuses on the adversities and refuses to acknowledge any positives. The second acknowledges the adversities but focuses on his learnings – the moments that have inspired him and what made him the superhero he is today.

Now, we aren't all superheroes in the traditional sense but we do all have moments in our lives that we can celebrate, however small, that have made us who we are. We have adversities that we have faced and conquered, and others we were scarred by. We have loves and losses, pain and joy, success and failure. It is how we tell those stories to ourselves that will affect how we feel about those stories. We don't need to see our lives through rose-tinted glasses, but we might want to reframe the power that we give those moments. 'Getting divorced ruined my life,' is one way to talk about a moment from the past and, 'I still don't think I'm over my divorce' is another. The first is finite, it is done. The storyteller will struggle to move forward because they have decided they can never recover from that moment. The second has the story still in action. It acknowledges the pain but suggests they are still processing that life moment – its affects are not yet finished and so neither is that particular story. This storyteller is moving forward, very slowly, as they loosen the grip that this particular episode has had on their life.

What stories are you giving power to? What adversities are you still holding onto? How can you reframe them so that they are not a burden you bear but rather a part of the story that shaped or is shaping you?

Once you have mastered telling your story so far, you can start to imagine your future stories. The shelves of books you are yet to write. You will notice when you are at the beginning of something, when the story is finished or when you know there's more just around the corner. Whether that is a change of career, the death of a loved one, a difficult patch in a relationship or just a funny story about the time you made dinner and accidentally set all the tea towels on fire, stories can be told so that we understand our own narrative and where we want that narrative to go. We can notice when bumps in the road have passed and enjoy offering up these little nuggets of our lives, like tasty morsels for our friends. We can mourn those who have passed by remembering stories about them. Stories are nourishment and sustenance for a life well-lived – we just need to get comfortable telling them.

Identifying Archetypes

I want to give you one last storytelling tool. In every story, there are characters and these fall into certain archetypes. When we are telling stories, particularly from our own lives, it can be helpful to identify these classic character roles that serve functions to keep the story moving along. When we recognise ourselves in archetypes, it can help us understand where we are in our own narrative and inform our decisions about what to do next. Below are definitions of the four most prominent archetypes, though there are several others (trickster and nemesis, for example). These four speak to me the most and appear regularly in my life. Perhaps you'll recognise them too.

Protagonist: The lead character whom the audience follow. We connect with their wishes and dreams and are carried with them on their journey: *Aladdin* (Disney's *Aladdin**) or Alice (*Alice in Wonderland*). Protagonists have to go through change – external and internal. If the protagonist doesn't learn, the journey isn't complete. If Jasmine said at the end of *Aladdin*, 'Sorry, I could just never love a street rat,' we would smash up the TV screen. We need her to love him for who he is because we have invested so much of ourselves in him.

To summarise: A protagonist is the lead character who goes on a literal or figurative journey. In your own story, this is you. In case that wasn't clear.

Antagonist: The force that is in the protagonist's way. This could be an evil nemesis: Jafar (*Aladdin*) or the Queen of Hearts (*Alice in Wonderland*). The difference between these two antagonists is that one is directly in conflict with the protagonist (Jafar wants to get rid of Aladdin) and the other is frustrated by the whole of the fantasy world (the Queen of Hearts is not that picky about who she shouts, 'Off with their head!' about). We can have an antagonist who wants to specifically get in our way or one that is getting in our way without aiming at us personally.

---

* Apologies, purists. I am an 80s kid. According to my brain, Disney wrote all the fairytales.

Classic antagonists in life are bullies in school or work, the boss who won't give you a day shift or the kid at school who wouldn't let you play with them. Antagonists that affect you indirectly can be economic fluctuation, racism, sexism (most of the '-isms'). These are not trying to stop you personally, but they are an obstacle to your journey.

Mentor: The person (or thing) that helps the protagonist on their way. The Genie (*Aladdin*) and the Caterpillar (*Alice in Wonderland*). The mentor character advises our protagonist about life, which the protagonist often dutifully ignores (see most of my boyfriends that my mum insinuated weren't as great as I thought they were). The mentor will often return later in the show to give the protagonist space to reflect on their learning having gone through some kind of trial. The Genie is the reverse of this trope, of course. Once Aladdin has learnt his lesson, he grants the Genie his freedom. Either way, the protagonist no longer needs them.

Think of parents, elders, therapists and bosses that have led you through a section of your life, culminating at a point where you no longer needed them in the same way. Some will disappear, some will transform into friends and some will simply fade into the background, not gone completely, but no longer needed to hold your hand.

Sidekick: This character is different to the mentor as the mentor is often further on in their life, whereas the sidekick is literally alongside the protagonist, assisting them on their journey. In Disney films, this is usually in the form of a funny animal. Aladdin's monkey, Abu, for example. He helps Aladdin out with his pilfering and listens to his concerns but it is clear to the audience that it is Aladdin's story. Alice doesn't have a sidekick (unless you count the White Rabbit, but he keeps running away) – she has to figure it all out by herself, poor chicken. In life, these are your friends, willing you along. The colleague who helps you with your work presentation, your buddy who gets you through a break-up, your partner who you choose to spend the rest of your life with.

Knowing these four basic archetypes will expand your storytelling ability. If we add them to our 'beginning, middle and end' concept, within a recognisable story shape, the story seems to take care of itself. Going back to your life story – which of these archetypes can you recognise? How did they affect you as a protagonist?

Collective Story Telling

Learning to improvise a story collectively is perhaps one of the hardest parts of improvisation to master and explains why I have left it till we are nearing the end of this book. It takes every single skill we have talked about so far and every drop of energy you can muster. In a glorious collective story, the group works seamlessly to create a nuanced and complex narrative, allowing each character to have their own sense of beginning, middle and end. The audience are on their feet and we, the performers, have had a transcendent experience, where we feel that perhaps we were channelling a story from another place altogether, rather than making it up. I have improvised over a thousand long-form narrative musicals with *Showstopper!*. We have managed to achieve this collective storytelling Utopia probably a hundred times. Ten per cent – not bad, eh?

To collectively create a narrative:

- We have to agree where we are in the story (beginning, middle or end).
- We have to ebb and flow with our offers, knowing when to play our offers and when to fold.
- We have to accept and work with each other's offers, even when they smash our personal plans.
- We have to pull together for the story even if the way we thought we were going suddenly disappears.

The tension in improvising a full narrative story is following our personal obvious, whilst relinquishing to the group mind. When we manage to mesh our individual mind within the group mind, we create something extraordinary. But it isn't easy, friends. It isn't easy. Have you ever had all your family want to go to a theme park and you just want to find a beach and have a swim? That's collective storytelling. Your family are pushing for their offer to be the platform in this chapter, and you are going to have to fold your offer of going to the beach, or go by yourself. When we learn to tell stories together, we are learning how to give and take, how to compromise, how to deal with frustration that stories don't go the way we want them to and we can either pack up and walk away or we can continue the story in the direction it's now being taken.

Life is one big improvised narrative, with many players coming in and out. I often see myself living many storylines – the sister, the daughter, the woman going to the shops, the wife, the woman arguing about the recycling, the friend trying to referee an argument between two other friends, the bad guy who hurt someone's feelings. I am the protagonist in my own story, yet someone else's mentor, a few people's sidekick and, every so often, the antagonist. When we see narrative shapes, we can map aspects of our lives onto them and review our stories to see if we can notice any common themes. Perhaps you have a lot of stories that end with you leaving a relationship. Or your stories might always involve you step-ping aside to let others move forward. Do you always 'do the right thing' but not seem to benefit from it? Are you in stories where you are the hero and others the sidekick? What story do your stories tell you about you?

I noticed about ten years ago that I had no stories about friends because I spent all my time working. All my anecdotes were based on jobs I was doing. They were funny, but I recog-nised a sadness in me when that realisation appeared. I spent some time making sure the next few stories in my library had tales of friendship and family in, so that when I looked back at that imaginary shelf, I would be satisfied by the narratives I had completed so far.

It is so easy to wander through life, not noticing your own stories, so have a go at writing your book titles. Take a pen and paper and write down significant stories in your life.

Relationships that affected you, events that shaped you, moments that have stayed with you. There can be as many as you like, although no less than ten. When you are finished, take a look at those titles and see a) what kinds of patterns you notice, b) what sorts of areas of your life don't seem to have as many chapters and c) what types of stories you might like to see in the future.

Triple Perspectives

Improvising narrative stories – longer pieces – takes a huge amount of focus on behalf of the players. We must not only be in the moment, noticing everything that is happening, but also outside of the moment, watching what is happening. This means that the improviser is not only able to apply tools and think about where the narrative is going, but also to notice where the narrative is, to be in that precise moment and fully present, yet also recognising how their character is developing, what offers are being made by others. It is juggling but rather than with balls, this clown has chosen multiple-levels of awareness. Awareness of self, of each other, of the world we are creating. It is the tension between these points that creates a great show. The artist, the mechanic and the director, working to make a story. And those three people are you.

When we co-create a story, we are asking ourselves to trust the other. We are, as performers, figuring out when to step forward and when to offer up space. Sometimes, we do these simultaneously. We have to navigate when it is our time to shine and when to shine light on others. For me, this is excellent training in life. Rather than simply learning how to stand out from the crowd, follow your passion, look after your own interests and tell your story, you also learn how to support others in their stories, when to back off and give them the spotlight and also, how to hold the spotlight together. How hard it is, in life, to dance with these nuances. To know how to work for the greater good and look after your own story simultaneously. Let's imagine our stories are all part of one greater story. And rather than be overwhelmed by the enormity of that task, let us try and be in the moment – improvise our way through the narrative, one beat at a time. Because trust me, it is so much simpler when you improvise.

Top Tips for Telling Your Own Stories

1. Don't try and tell your complete life story all at once – if we start at the trip down the birth canal, it's going to be a long day. Choose the focus point and build your story around that.

2. Know what you want from the story. Want to make people laugh? Want to share an embarrassing moment? Is it a more tender, vulnerable share? If you know what your desired outcome is, you'll better know which story to tell.

3. Connect to how you felt at the time and tell us about that. Were you angry? Sad? Happy? Confused? All the

above? The more we connect to the emotion behind the story to the moments or plot points in the story, the more engaged your audience will be. Don't just tell us that the car wouldn't start – tell us how it made you feel.

4. The more time has passed since a story happened, the easier it usually is to tell it. We can see it more fully. If someone dumped you yesterday, today may not be the time to tell that story to someone you just met.

5. Enjoy telling your stories. Take pride in the tales of your life. If you aren't enjoying it, it will be harder for your audience to.

6. If telling stories on the spot makes you nervous, start by having a few you have thought of in advance. If we practise writing down stories, we will eventually find it easier to make them up.

Exercise Corner

SOLO

Tell your own story up to now. You can write it out or record it as a voice note. Read or listen to it back. How do you tell your story? Are you the protagonist*? Who have been the antagonists in your life? What have been your high and your low points?

Now think about the next chapter in your story. Again, take maybe five minutes and write/record the story of the next ten years. What do you dream of? What do you hope for you, your community, the world? Remember, this is an imagination exercise, so achievability does not have to come into it yet. If you want to imagine a solution to flooding in the Midlands or everyone with enough food and drink and a roof over their head, you can. If you want to imagine space travel with unicorns, go for it. Only by allowing us to imagine the impossible can we get closer to finding the possible.

IN A PAIR

Tell your life story to your partner. Give yourself a two-minute time limit. Your partner then has to repeat back to you what

---

* You'd be amazed how many people are not the protagonists when telling their own stories. Make sure you are talking about you in this exercise first and any additional characters, second.

you told them in 60 seconds. If they have missed anything or you realise you have left anything out, you can add things back in (for example, I once had someone in a workshop who realised he had only talked about academic achievements and forgotten to mention his wife and two children). Finally, the person who has listened to the story, tells it back to you as a fairy-tale, starting 'Once upon a time . . .'

Notice how you feel, hearing your story. What things leap out at you? How has your partner interpreted your story?

IN A GROUP

If you have three or four pals to play with (and this may seem like an odd thing to suggest to do at the pub or at Costa Coffee but see what happens) then try to make up a story together. Have a sentence each. Try to find a beginning, a middle and an end whilst discovering which archetypes appear. Notice how easy it is to expand that Circle of Ideas to include so many elements, that it then becomes impossible to reincorporate them all. Most importantly, if it goes a bit bonkers, laugh and start again. Fail beautifully at creating these stories and then suddenly, one will seem perfect to you. It will feel satisfying and you will collectively know when it is finished, without having to ask.

The Art of Shelving

Sometimes, in an improvised show, you make an offer on stage that is not for that immediate moment. It is an idea that the improviser believes is relevant to the story they are telling but not something to be acted on right there and then, so we 'shelve it' i.e. put it on an imaginary shelf to return to at a later date, if needed. It is different to folding an idea, which is to say goodbye to an idea permanently for the good of the show. This is a suggestion that is lightly placed up on an imaginary shelf for us to come back to if we want.

For example, the show is set in a dive bar and one character says, 'My Grandma used to run a bar.' The characters then move on to a completely different topic (that is how you collectively know it has been shelved – no one is curious about that idea, it is not deepened, it is moved on from). The offer is either never mentioned again (because the story went in a different direction), becomes a point of interest a bit later ('Didn't your Grandma run a bar once?') or ties up the whole darn show ('I can't believe Grandma fixed the beer pump and saved the bar!'). The improvisers won't know what the offer is for when they make it, but they will recognise that it has been 'shelved' not 'folded'.

Every day we have ideas of things we might like to do, places we might like to go, ambitions we might like to fulfil. Shelving is a great way to look at these. They are ideas we have that we want to explore but now might not be the time. This does not mean the idea has to be dismissed but rather it is left for a future you. A future you who has time to give this idea the attention it deserves or a future you who can reassess the idea and think: 'Why did I want to do that?' Maybe you have a creative idea you wish to pursue but now is not the time. Shelve it. Maybe you want to travel but now is not the time. Shelve it. We are not giving up on our dreams, we are shelving them for a time when they might be better supported.

WHAT HAPPENS NEXT?

In improvisation, we say you can only judge a scene when it's finished. Therefore, you can only judge a moment when it is over and you can only judge a book when you are on the last page. And here we are, nearing the very end of our journey together. So take a moment. Think about what has struck you as interesting. If you did the exercises, what revelations did you have, no matter how small? Can you imagine ways this could shift your perspective in the day-to-day, the hour-to-hour or the year-to-year? The book coming to an end doesn't mean your journey with improv has ended, in fact, I hope it has just begun. You have some tools: now it's time to go out into the world and use them. I am so excited for you.

In the spirit of improvisation, what happens next is up to you and it is only your *next* step you need to think about. The rest will follow. Perhaps you are going to keep working on your YES and your NO. You might wish to go back to thinking about your story and how you want the next chapter to unfold. Maybe you are going to focus on your eye contact and being more present with the people around you. Perhaps you are going to join a workshop and explore these processes in a group setting. Pick one step and make a habit of it. Keep a diary – notice what impact this work has.

Bumbag of Tools

By reaching the end of this book, you are now equipped with the following:

- Noticing your use of YES and NO.
- Asking yourself, 'Who are you? Where are you? What are you doing?'
- Being curious about the world around you and the choices you are making.
- Following your obvious.
- Listening to your body.
- Checking in with your eye contact.
- Hearing the offers of your friends, family and the universe.
- Noticing status transactions.
- Giving up control.
- Knowing when to step forward and when to step back.
- Being willing to fail, as long as you are willing to learn.
- Telling your own story with a beginning, a middle and an end.
- Placing yourself in narratives that differ to your own, working with the imagination to hold bigger, inspiring visions for yourself and your fellow humans*.

---

* That's a meaty one. Enjoy getting your teeth into that (vegan option available).

You can apply these tools in the smallest way: playing with your kids, exploring creativity in the workplace, thinking about the quality of the offers you are giving to people in your life.

You can apply it to bigger life moments: how present you are in your relationships or what career opportunities you want to say YES to. What has your gut been telling you that you've been pushing to the side? What have you been frightened of failing at that has stopped you even taking the first step?

Finally, you can apply them in an expansive way: how can we explore change within our worlds with these tools? How can we remain curious as a nation with each new challenge the universe throws at us? How can all the countries of the world co-create the future together, embracing the individuality of each nation whilst working towards a common goal? These may seem bold, fantastical plans, but why not? Improv asks us not to stay in the status quo but wonder 'What if . . .?' – as do all groups asking for change. Improv asks us to listen to all the offers, and not just the ones we like. Not just the ones that are easy. An improv mindset widens out the world and then challenges us to ask questions, whilst moving forward.

Do the Work

I was leading a workshop in a law firm, as I often do, talking about listening. Whilst explaining an exercise, one of the participants said, 'So if I do this, I can make my client think I am listening to them?' I thought this a most revealing sentence. I replied, 'Even better, it will help you actually listen to them*.' So often when I am teaching this work, people are looking for this kind of shortcut. The ability to give the impression of working as a team, of listening, of collaborating, without actually having to do any of these things. Unfortunately, there are no shortcuts. You've got to do the work and there will be things you need to change. Embrace the change. Enjoy the revelations that exercises bring. Practise the exercises with people you trust, apply one principle at a time (to avoid being overwhelmed) and laugh. Oh my goodness, please, laugh. While we do this work on ourselves, we must find joy in each other and ourselves. Life should not be a slog, though it can feel like it sometimes. Anywhere we can fit in a giggle, a smirk and laugh-till-you-are-crying moment is welcome because goodness knows we are going to face hardships and sadness along the way. Let us be open to the good stuff, too.

An Improviser's Journey

When I first started improvising, it was because I wanted to be funny. I was pretty funny, but I wanted to be able to be funny with other people, to make funny scenes with them and cause crowds to fall over, laughing. With the tools of Who What

---

* Mic drop moment. If this were a film, there would be a close-up on the participant, who would realise what they'd been missing all this time. Then I would open my umbrella and fly into the clouds. Unfortunately, it was real life, so they just wrinkled their nose and went back to their BlackBerry.

Where and YES AND, noticing my blocking and being sure of what my face was doing, I was able to do that. I was able to say, 'I made those people laugh'. This is a great reason to do improv – to make people laugh. To connect with the audience and your teammates, and bring joy and play into the world.

A few years into improvising, I learnt the valuable lesson of making my partner look good. That, rather than focusing on myself, I could spend my time on stage doing whatever was possible to get my scene buddy's eyes to light up. I could take pleasure in *their* performance, rather than focusing on my own. This was an important step, and one I couldn't have taken without having had that first step of being comfortable with my own abilities. Once I wasn't worrying about the basics, I could focus on other people. I could get my joy fix *with* them rather than through them.

A few more years into improvising, I had learnt narrative structures and I learnt to see where stories could go whilst being in the moment. To imagine and adapt. In the same way I needed to know and trust myself and my skills before I could truly support my fellow improviser. We recognised that we needed to know and trust our characters to get a richer, more satisfying story.

That is what this book is about – knowing and trusting yourself so you can make bold choices, whilst listening and collaborating with your fellow humans. The ability to bring your full self into situations and not be frightened that you are not enough or that you are too much.

When I started teaching improvisation, it was to help students become better, more intuitive performers (and how to instantly create a kick-ass song on a dime). Now it has expanded to the stage of life – to people who don't want to be actors. Showing that non-actors also need to embrace themselves and their creativity fully, practise living in uncertainty and discover what it is to be an individual within a team. How to hold the paradox of our personal wishes within the group experience. To follow our heart's desire whilst staying in tune with our communities. To discover the group desire, together. Improv Your Life became a course for people to work on themselves and how they want to be in the world.

So my final question is this: What is the world you want to leave behind? In improvisation we create whole narratives from our imaginations. We describe mountain ranges whilst standing in a rehearsal room, we give a vision of Utopia whilst wearing our weekend jeans. The gift that improvisation gives us is access to the collective imagination.

By working on your imagination through improvisation, you will be able to imagine your future self and the world you want to live in. What opportunities do you want to see for us as a human race? What shapes and ways of life might you like to change? Can you imagine what that might look like? For when we can see it in our mind's eye, we are closer to making it real. Parker Palmer's Centre for Courage and Renewal states: 'It remains possible for us, young and old alike, to find our voices, learn how to speak them, and know the satisfaction that comes from contributing to positive change.'

What is Your Desire?

When you go for a walk in a park, through fields or any green space, there are these little paths where you can see many people have realised it makes more sense to walk in a certain direction, rather than follow the council's approved way. The grass is worn and a new path has been created. Humans have improvised a new route by following their obvious and placing one foot in front of the other. These tracks are known in planning circles as 'desire paths'. The people act out their desire and a new lane is made. Often, councils will incorporate them into the official path system during their next tidy up, recognising that the people have spoken. Some councils will do everything they can to try to stop people going off the official track: red and white tape, fencing, 'keep off the grass' signs. Yet we persevere, though some may 'tut', because we know it makes no sense to follow the *prescribed* path. The path that was created perhaps without consultation. A path made for aesthetics rather than practicality. We need to question our paths. To find our own desire paths. If we are onto something, others will follow. My deepest hope is that you find your voice, speak up for yourself and for others, and you see positive change in tiny ways that forge a new path. A path you didn't know you wanted to follow but seems completely obvious once you are there.

May improvisation give you the courage to take your space in the world, forge your path and follow your obvious into new and exciting places, right on your doorstep. We have an abundance inside of us. When we are able to access our abundance, we realise the riches of the world were inside us all along. Keep shifting the edge of your comfort zone. Expand it, inch by inch, until you find the real boundaries, rather than those that were bestowed upon you.

We have no idea what is going to happen globally in the next five years, let alone fifty, which means we need to be ready to adapt, to accept change and know ourselves inside out. We need to be ready to speak with our neighbours, to move forward even when in conflict and find different ways to approach new and repeating issues. We need to be able to do all these things whilst laughing, dancing and embracing the fullness of life in all its messy glory.

Improv is the art of being OK when the plan takes an unexpected turn.

Improv is the art of trusting your skills and your gut.

Improv is the art of knowing yourself and being able to work in relationship with others.

Improv is the art of failing forwards by embracing and reframing wisdom which appears in the form of a mistake.

Improv is the art of YES and NO and all that lies between.

Improv is being able to leave the space and know you have given all you can to that moment.

Improv is celebrating the brilliance of others without feeling that it diminishes your own.

Improv is a world that is accessible to all, embracing of fear and full of hope. For without hope, we cannot improvise.

Everything you need is inside yourself, it just takes a while to find it.

Good luck, fellow improviser.

Remember – the work is never done.
We are always growing and changing and learning.
Let this be inspiring rather than daunting.
You never have to be stuck.

This is like the secret track on *Jagged Little Pill* . . .

'The Glorious Idiot' (a post-revelation poem)
by Pippa Evans

I AM AN IDIOT!
It took me a while to realise.
Because I got told – 'Don't be an idiot!'
So even though I had an inkling
that I might be an idiot –
I did what I was told and tried to be
anything other than an idiot.
I'd say 'I knew that!' or
'I read that, like, a year ago!' or
'Really? You think THAT? You must be an idiot!'
Oh how I judged and mocked those idiots
till my stomach was knotted with miserable, arrogant
     sneers
and my head was dizzy from towering over those
     joyful, inquisitive idiots.
Then, one day, I awoke and thought:
YOU IDIOT!
You are killing yourself trying NOT to be an idiot!!!
So I say to you – 'I AM AN IDIOT!'
Oh, what freedoms since embracing my idiot self!
Idiots ask questions . . . and listen to the answers!
Idiots say 'Thank you' and 'Please' and 'How are you?'
Idiots make mistakes . . . and admit them. And
     apologise.
Idiots are happy to sit in the unknown. To watch the
     world pass by

and sweep them up and go around them,

sat in the centre, taking it all in,

not always knowing what it means or even if it
    means anything at all.

Idiots keep eating pastries even though they know
    they are full.

I want to be my best self.

And my best self is an idiot.

A glorious idiot!

A beautiful, stupid, clever, hideous, amazing idiot.

Before I embraced my idiot I would say,

'I know everything!'

Wearing it like a protective shield.

So I proudly say,

'I know nothing!'

Everything I learn teaches me there is more to learn.

So I ask you – will you be an idiot with me?

Then let us rise up

and become the wisest, kindest, strongest group of
    idiots

this world has ever seen.

But only, of course, if you are an idiot.

And if you're not an idiot then forgive me for mistak-
    ing you.

For I AM AN IDIOT!

ACKNOWLEDGEMENTS

Thank goodness for other people – so many wonderful, generous folk have helped bring this book to life. Firstly, all the people at Hodder Studio who took a chance on publishing a book about improv, especially Myfanwy Moore, who kept me going during lockdown and Bea Fitzgerald who didn't blink when I added yet another quote that needed to be checked. Also, thanks to Hannah Chambers, Katy Eyre and the Chambers Management gang, who continue to be the best agents in the land.

So many performers and improvisers were generous with their time and knowledge when I approached them, especially Heather Urqhuart, Jennifer Lack, Neil Mullarkey, Lee Simpson, Phillip Pellew, Mark Womersley, Monica Gaga, Minder Kaur Athwal, Maria Peters, Chloe Kennedy, Francesca Reid, Luke Sorba, Sean McCann, Stella Duffy, Judith Jacob, Luke Sorba, Eleanor Tiernan, Suki Webster, Peta Lily, Ian McLaughlin, Patti Stiles and Lucy Trodd who spoke to me on the phone, read chapters or just encouraged me when I was having a wobble.

To my wise friends Mark Vernon, Cat White, Olivia Hamlyn, Vanessa Chamberlain, Siva Thambisetty, Elizabeth Oldfield, Anthea Lawson, Chris Oldfield, Jules Evans and Johnathan

Rowson who helped me with quotes, spelling, thoughts and general encouragement. I am sure you will miss your WhatsApp notifications pinging, now that the book is done.

My fellow Showstoppers who teach me something every time we meet and without whom the last 12 years would not have been anywhere near as exciting. Thank you for your skill, your generosity and your hilariousness when we are improvising yet another musical set in Ikea. May there be a thousand more musicals for us to discover, together.

The hundreds of inspiring folks I have met at various improv festivals around the world have been an invaluable source of wonder and offered me space to explore and percolate some of the ideas in this book, especially Det Andre Teatret of Oslo, Norway, Rapid Fire Theatre and Die-Nasty of Edmonton, Canada, Würzberg Festival, Germany and I Bugiardini of Rome, Italy.

All the participants of Improv Your Life who have contributed to the writing of this book – especially Kathryn Pintus who offered to do a punctuation pass of the manuscript (I now almost understand commas) – thank you all for your bravery in the room and your willingness to experiment with new ideas, bringing yourself into the space and trusting me with your experiences. Thank you to Sunday Assembly, especially Sanderson Jones, Ruth Moir and Marla Dufek, for giving me the space and encouragement to start the adventure with my Improv Your Life classes.

Thanks to Adam Megiddo and Alan Marriott who taught me so much about improvisation and saw a spark worth encouraging. Keith Johnstone and Viola Spolin – thank you for getting the improv ball rolling. All of us are indebted to you and your boldness.

To Mum and Dad, for being encouraging when I have gone down yet another path you weren't expecting, my brothers who are always proud of my seemingly strange choices and Mr Bunce, who loves me even when I am singing improvised songs at 2am in the living room.

And to the many improv shows that have been and gone.

May there be many more where you came from.

ABOUT THE AUTHOR

Pippa Evans is an award-winning musical performer, song-writer and improviser. As a solo musical comedy performer, she was nominated for Best Newcomer at the Edinburgh Comedy Awards, and has performed comedy across the world, including the Montreal Just for Laughs Festival and the Melbourne Comedy Festival.

As a core member of the Olivier award-winning *Showstopper! The Improvised Musical*, Pippa has toured the UK and internationally. She is a series regular on Radio 4's *The Now Show* and has appeared on ITV's *Tonight at the Palladium*. She is the dramaturg on **9 to 5:** *The Musical* at the Savoy Theatre and wrote the finale to *The Jack Whitehall Christmas Special* at the London Palladium. Pippa co-hosts *The Showstopper! Podcast*, and created and hosts *Parts I'll Never Play* at The Other Palace. As an actor she most recently appeared in *The End Of the F***ing World* for Channel 4 and Netflix.

Pippa co-created and performs in two improv groups: *The Glenda J Collective* (alongside Josie Lawrence, Cariad Lloyd and Ruth Bratt) and *There Will Be Cake* (alongside Marcus Brigstocke, Rachel Parris and Paul Foxcroft). Both groups have performed sell-out runs at the Edinburgh Fringe Festival and at London's Soho Theatre.

Pippa also developed and leads a course entitled Improv Your Life in which she demonstrates how improv can be applied to everyday life. Pippa's improv teaching has been featured in both *The Telegraph* and *The Guardian*.

She also created Sunday Assembly, a weekly church for people who don't believe in God.

Improv Your Life is Pippa's first book.